Doc's
Poetry Parlor

Andre Lawrence

Doc's Poetry Parlor

Copyright © 2021 by Andre Lawrence

All rights reserved. No part of this publication may be reproduced, distributed, or transmitted in any form or by any means, including photocopying, recording, or other electronic or mechanical methods, without the prior written permission of the author, except in the case of brief quotations embodied in critical reviews and certain other non-commercial uses permitted by copyright law.

ISBN
978-1-956529-18-0 (Paperback)
978-1-956529-17-3 (eBook)

I would like to dedicate this book to my family, friends, children (and their mothers), and to every person that has opened their heart to me and allowed me to take refuge within.

I have met so many uniquely inspiring individuals along my journey in this life who have inspired me.

I want to say I love you and I thank you for bestowing your trust in me.

Sincerely,
Andre "Doc" Lawrence.

Table of Contents

The Prelude: Come and Go Love 1
The Foolish Man 4
You Are Woman 6
She Is 8
Honduranean Rose 10
Woman Unknown 12
I Bear Witness 14
Black Butterfly 16
This Love 18
My Black Is Beautiful 20
The Beauty of Love 22
Under the Guidance of Time 24
Family 26
Before the Council of Men 28
The Afterthought to Forward Thinking 30
Apologetic Father 32
In This Life 34
I Am Thee 36
Me and My Destiny 38
It Has Been an Honor 40
Hear Ye, Hear Ye (All You Battle-Ready Souls) 42
Cannibal Mentality 46
Sign of the Times 48
All that My Eyes Have Seen 50

Real Nigga Rich	52
Bully Me Not	54
The Letter	56
We Interrupt the Regularly Scheduled Program	58
In the Wake of Summer	60
American-Less	62
Social Address	64
I Have a Clear View through My Window	66
I Wonder, Will They Listen?	68
This Road	70
Rizin' against the Oddss	72
Tragic Reality	74
This Is My Pain Eulogized	76
The Incline of Injustice	80
Rivers of Blood	82
These Are the Tears I Cry	84
Bad Times upon Us	86
Ye though I Walk	88
America's Outcast	92
They Say that I Am a Racist	94
US Occupation	96
The Cruel Truth	98
Today We Gather	100
History's Present	102
Am I Not Worthy?	104
New Thought, New Man	106
I Am a Human Being	110
The Day Freedom Came	112
Justice or Else	114
I Am the Undesirable—Part 1	116
I Am the Undesirable—Part 2	118
I Am	120
The Darkness in which I Dwell	122

Strong Black Soul	124
I Am Powerful	126
A Man Trying to Get Right with God	128
The Vowing Man	130
Atonement	132
From theSidelines	134
The Will of Concepts	136
Time, the Revealer	138
Belizean Queen	140
Forever My White Girl	142
Sue Mama	144
Pride of Tennessee	146
Here's to the Couple	148
Tasha Brown	150
Gratitude	152
On this Day	154
Farewell, Linde	156
Juneteenth	158
If Heaven Could Hear Me	160
Kwanzaa	166
Farewell, FMC	168
Nurse Appreciation Week	170
The Dearly Departed Son	172
A Mother I Have Never Met	174
Eternally Whitney	176
In Memory of Li'l Arthur	178
O Mother My	180
In Memory of Rachel	182
Dearly Beloved	184
Trina Lives	186
The Last of the Leading Ladies	188
Time after Time	190
Eternally Uncle Lewis	192

I Am Muhammad Ali	194
In Loving Memory of Li'l Greg	196
Breathing through the Storm	198
Mildred's Son	200
Before the Heavenly Trumpet Blows	202
In the Blink of an Eye	204
Let It Be Said	206
I Am Still Here	208
Endlessly Fateful	210
Alone with My Thoughts	212
Look at Me	214
Love's Devotion	216
Loving You in Hindsight	218
One-Sided Love	220
A Song to Memory	222
Senses	224
Fears of Love	226
I Need You	228
Hello, Love	230
Hearts Broken Silence	232
I Am Torn	234
Dreamland	236
Tell Me	238
Dual Inspiration	240
Where Are You Headed?	242
What Will My Legacy Be?	246
I Am Atoning	250
Still I Rize	252
A Tribute to Woman	254
The Black Woman	258
Poetic Response to Li'l Baby	260
The Familiar Stranger	262

Foreword

I want to first give thanks and praise to the Most High God, who is the creator of all that is, who saw it fit to give me life and instilled in me my purpose. Second, I'd like to extend my gratitude and thanks to my family, beginning with my mother, Debra Lawrence Murphy, who, from as early as I can remember, always made me aware that I was special; may you rest in peace, Momma. Then there is my sister and brothers, who have always shown their faith in me and supported me in this life. Sarina, Jesse (RIP), Johnny, and Josh, our love lives in action Continually, and I thank you all dearly. I am truly honored to be called brother, and to all my children, I can only say, you all were the beginning of the best of me coming forth, because you gave me a new sense of direction. To the women bore my children, I thank you for helping me maintain a family unit among the children and enduring those rough patches along the way. Last, to my friends, some of which have grown closer than blood, loyalty is the code we abide under and has been undeniably on display in those times I needed you most; I sincerely thank you. So to all of you who have made an impact on my life, I pray this book will bear a reflection of a man worthy to be honored in the manner in which you have honored me, and to my new reading audience, I hope you will find this book full of the inspiration for which it was written.

Most sincerely,

Andre "Doc" Lawrence
The author

The Prelude: Come and Go Love

The person you're trying to reach is unavailable. Please leave a message after the beep.

Hello, love,
    it's me
calling you to address some things.

But it seems you're unavailable
    while my world's unstable,
so I guess I'll just talk to this damn machine.

First, let me take us
    back to the start
where our journey begins,

Recalling the bliss
    of love anew,
to its presently tragic end.

First contact,
    our eyes deadlock,
and not a word did we dare to speak.

It was in that instance
    you became my mission
with hopes of making you mine to keep.

With my ambition as fuel,
    I pursued with purpose
to have you before the dawning sun.

I guess fate had a hand
    and forced life circumstance,
leaving me the victor; the prize of you I won.

And what a slow romance
    we did indulge,
savoring each moment that passed.

We talked;
    we made love
and continued this course as if it were our last.

And oh, how fate
    can play a cruel game
as we managed from state to state.

You were the valley girl,
    and I'm city boy slick;
we found love but only got a taste.

And just as you would imagine,
    the unthinkable happened;
I'm ushered to a foreign place.

No message in advance
    to ease your concerns.
I'm gone without a trace.

But through common grounds
    of those we know,
our communication got back on track.

And no words could express
    the feelings I felt
when I thought I had you back.

Communication once again broken,
    no words between us spoken,
so this void leaves my lonely heart sore.

And it seems you keep
    jumping in and out of my life
using my heart as a revolving door.

But let the record reflect
    no matter how many times you come and go,
a piece of you I'll always yearn.

And though you're gone for the moment
    for who knows how long,
I patiently await your return.

End of Message

Uniquely worded by
Andre "Doc" Lawrence

The Foolish Man

Taking a moment
    to reflect on this life
and all the love we shared,

I knew from the beginning
    that you were the one
and no other would compare.

You stole my heart
    without the use of force,
and my best interest you always held.

But being the foolish man,
    I often gave reason
that caused you to scream and yell.

From our encounter
    'til this present day,
that love we built remains.

And no unseen force
    could ever undo
what my heart will never change.

I know in times past
    I played the fool
and made decisions beyond the risk.

In the pursuit of my goals,
    I never could fathom
an outcome quite like this.

One that has left me
    alone and away
from you and our children as well.

Yet in my time away,
    I can only pray you'll forgive;
of this only time will tell.

Having had a moment to reflect
    and assess my life,
on this position I have to stand.

You gave so much
    that I took for granted;
I am the foolish man.

Uniquely worded by
Andre "Doc" Lawrence

You Are Woman

You are the beginning
    of all that is
every man that walks this earth.

You are the first protector,
    teacher, and provider
and remained so since the time of birth.

Your unfailing love
    knows no limit,
and your pain you'd barely show.

You even forgave
    in our moments of rage
when we foolishly abused youso.

Instead of love in return,
    you were repaid with brute force
in an attempt to break your will.

And yet even in our filth
    and shameful state,
you proudly proclaimed us still.

There's no mountain high
    or valley low
that could deter you from your course.

And of all the gold,
    Oil, and water in the world,
you're the most precious natural resource.

You are the crown jewel
    more than worthy of praise
to whom all honor is due.

And every head should bow
    when in the midst of your presence
as a sign of respect toward you.

    You are woman . . .

Uniquely worded by
Andre "Doc" Lawrence

She Is

She is the ideal woman
    that other women aspire
and no man has ever tamed.

She is a force of nature
    whose love knows no bounds
and heart has never been claimed.

She is the candy-lick whisperer
    behind the soothing voice
that comforts the wounded soul.

She is the battle-scarred matriarch
    from the times of ancient
whose mysteries remain untold.

She is honor and loyalty
    embodied in flesh
whose spirit is pure and true.

She is the prototype
    of every man's delight
to which respect is always due.

If I could list the achievements
    and all the great things
that this woman has ever did,

I would give you an image
    of a godlike figure,
and to me, she truly is.

    She is!

Uniquely worded by
Andre "Doc" Lawrence

Honduranean Rose

There's not a day that passes
    that the thought of you
ceases to cross my mind.

And with thought come memories
    of moments we shared
and days of happier times.

What we had was beautiful,
    and I never had a problem
doing whatever to make you shine.

But due to your past
    and pain unresolved,
I begin to suffer with the course of time.

But like every relationship,
    we had our ups and downs,
and we maintained as best we could.

You had your ways,
    and I had my pride,
but we're still here, so it's all good.

They say time will tell,
    you live and you learn,
but it's only God who truly knows.

Claudia, from me to you,
    the love is still here,
and you'll always be my Honduranean tose.

Uniquelyworded by
Andre "Doc"Lawrence

Inspired by
Phil

Woman Unknown

Caught up in thought
    over this woman unknown,
my mind continues to race.

For I only have a description,
    so I'm forced to imagine
what beauty lies in wait.

In a six-foot frame
    clothed in chocolate skin
that I'm sure is soft to touch,

With this as an image,
    you must forgive me
for whatever thoughts I have of lust.

Because being the man I am,
    I must stay mindful
to pursue with class and grace

and not create a situation
    where you become uncomfortable
and give you cause to back away.

I'm not looking for love,
    and maybe you're not either,
but let's play the hand we're dealt.

And what will be,
    let it be so
and just enjoy the experience of someone else.

So in my closing remarks,
    I think it's only fair that you know
that I'll be me from beginning to end.

And for whatever the case,
    our paths have crossed;
I hope to have gained a friend.

Uniquely worded by
Andre "Doc" Lawrence

I Bear Witness

I bear witness to the truth
    of the woman you are
and the beauty that lies within.

Though you make no attempt
    to allow the world to see you,
my eyes see beneath the skin.

And what a lovely sight
    it is to behold,
and in your presence, you'll always find me.

You're like a hidden treasure
    in the depths of the sea
that brings joy to the one that finds thee.

I bear witness to this truth
    because the truth it is
and will always be forever true.

And you can take these words
    for all they're worth;
another woman ain't got nothing on you.

Uniquely worded by
Andre "Doc" Lawrence

Black Butterfly

Like the morning sun,
    you chose to rise,
leaving behind all the darkened nights.

And against the odds,
    you chose your fate;
you would endure, stand, and fight.

For each struggle you faced,
    you did it with grace
and never veered off track.

You soared the skies
    with wings of an angel
with no fear of looking back.

There were many life lessons
    learned from your conception,
and it's evident you were meant to be.

You evolved from your cocoon,
    a blossoming beauty
for all the world to see.

From the ashes of nothingness,
    you became a monument of praise;
of this we cannot deny.

Though your form has changed
    and you were given many names,
you are the black butterfly.

Uniquely worded by
Andre "Doc" Lawrence

This Love

How do I describe
    this love divine
And all that I feel
    in this heart of mine?

Through every test,
    trial, and pain combined,
this love hasmanaged
    to somehow shine.

No rain, sleet,
    or winter's cold
could force a break
    in this love's grip hold.

This love is indescribable,
    undeniable, unchangeable,
and underrated.

But more importantly,
    this love
has been highly underestimated.

Uniquely worded by
Andre "Doc" Lawrence

My Black Is Beautiful

My Black is beautiful;
    like the morning sun,
there's nothing that can stop my shine.

And like the sun's rays,
    I'm a blend of multishades,
and there's no other beauty that compares to mine.

I am a descendant of greatness
    that has hailed areign
since the times ofancient.

I am the first of mothers
    whom Africa bore
and gave birth to a mighty nation.

I am the warrior queen,
    and my show of strength
is not in the war I make.

But my true show of power
    is displayed in that final hour
when I can lean on nothing but my faith.

My black is beautiful
    and second to none
and more precious than the finest gold.

And it's endowed with an essence
    that has transcended time
and is also fierce and bold.

My black is beautiful

Uniquely worded by
Andre "Doc" Lawrence

The Beauty of Love

The beauty of love,
    as I have come to learn,
It exists because it is
    but guarantees no return.

Though accompanied with pain,
    it brings so much joy
And is incurable despite
    the remedies we employ.

So for the shattered hearts
    and tormented souls,
Who have tasted this love
    but lost your hold,

I would encourage you this
    as you sojourn:
Deny not that love
    in you so burn.

For it is birth from a time
    before time begin
And continues a course
    that will never end.

And to have known this love
    you know now what's true,
That it is and expands
    beyond the realm of you.

So just embrace the love
    you have come to know,
And if it should return,
    never let it go.

Uniquely worded by
Andre "Doc" Lawrence

Under the Guidance of Time

Under the guidance of time,
    I grew from a young mustard seed
to a firmly rooted tree.

And no matter the storms
    that constantly came,
there was no uprooting me.

See I was planted knee-deep
    in the soil of concrete,
so just to be was an amazing feat.

And the fact that I am
    solidifies the point
that I am certainly meant to be.

Under the guidance of time,
    having endured thus far,
I wait patiently for the coming rains,

For though the storms have quieted
    and the sun shines brightly,
I know the weather is soon to change.

But until it does,
    I will extend my branches
and grow taller for the world to see

And deepen my roots
    within this concrete soil
to ensure there's no removing me.

Uniquely worded by
Andre "Doc" Lawrence

Family

I'm mindful each day
    as each new day begins
To let love rule the day
    from beginning to end,

To keep family and friends
    within arm's length,
For when life's trials come,
    they are my support and strength,

That I may never lose sight
    along this journey's road
And remain honorable at all times
    for the truth I hold.

For I am bound by more
    than the blood in my veins
Or the ideals and beliefs
    that will never change.

Because the bond that mends
    is our centerpiece,
Passed on from me to you
    and bloodline deep,

It will be tested and tried
    but will never break
And has endured from the beginning
    'til this present day.
We are what we are,
    and some will never be;
Be it blood or covenant,
    we are family.

Uniquely worded by
Andre "Doc" Lawrence

Before the Council of Men

Today I stand
    before the council of men,
Who weigh in the balance
    my wages of sin.

For crimes and deeds
    and claims of acts,
I endured the punishment
    without lashing back,

Because truly I knew
    the day would come
That from this state
    the Lord would deliver me from.

So with my faith
    and sound mind, I stand,
Ready to fulfill
    my purpose and plan,

Because bravely I stood
    before the council of men,
Who knew not my story
    or how it would end,

Whose very intent
    was to weaken me so
That I might surrender
    and never grow.

But they have never known
    the man who stands,
For had they known,
    they would've changed their plans

And not pursued
    the likes of me,
Because a man I stand
    and will always be.

Uniquely worded by
Andre "Doc" Lawrence

The Afterthought to Forward Thinking

From the moment of the last click
    of the handcuffs on my wrist,
life for me had changed,

And all that I knew
    and the things I used to do
cease to be the same.

No more gathering with friends
    and partying nights on end;
my former life is gone.

I've been deemed suitably fit
    by the powers that be
and placed in a wasting zone.

With no recourse of action
    to undo my fate,
I endure with a mind of peace,

Trusting wholly with heart,
    mind, body, and soul
that God will grant release

But waiting patiently for that moment
    that my resurrection shall come,
for with me shall come relief.

And I'll bring with me joy
    in exchange for tears
and put an end to the blood in our streets.

Uniquely worded by
Andre "Doc" Lawrence

Apologetic Father

It has become quite apparent
    and painfully obvious
that my memory is starting to fail.

To what extent,
    I do not know;
only time will tell.

But rest assured,
    my darling daughter,
I never meant to upset you so.

And the shame I feel
    for forgetting your age,
the pain you'll never know.

For as your father,
    I'm held accountable
for all I say and do.

And I can only ask
    that you forgive me this
and how it affected you,

For great is the pain
    a father will suffer
when at odds with his child.

And no matter how small,
    no remedy will do
until they are fully reconciled.

Uniquely worded by
Andre "Doc" Lawrence

In This Life

In this life I have lived,
    so much I have seen
and value every experience gained,

Though there have been moments of distress
    and times I didn't reflect my best,
but each day brings a new day of change.

In this life,
    I endured my portion
of suffering joy and pain,

But each pain-filled moment
    was followed by joy renewed,
so I will not complain.

In this life for me,
    sacrifice wascommon,
but I did it with no regret.

I became the lamb
 who would bathe the altar in blood
for those who hadn't made it yet.

In this life, I am a student
 whose constant study
is mastering the art of me.

Though there be thousands of books
 and countless lessons,
none has taught me how to be.

In this life, I am determined
 to defy the odds
and keep my purpose always in view.

And no matter the storms that come,
 I will not yield
but fulfill what I am meant to do.

Uniquely worded by
Andre "Doc" Lawrence

I Am Thee

If I told you once,
    I told you a thousand times,
I am thee
    and another me you'll never find.

Search as you wish
    among the shell of men
And you will only come
    to an exhausting end.

For of the chosen men,
    in me favor was found,
And my presence is felt
    even when I am not around.

I am desired by kings,
    but the queens delight,
And I will be envied more in death
    than I am in life.

So hear me clearly,
    these words I speak:
I am thee,
    and another me will never be.

Uniquely worded by
Andre "Doc" Lawrence

Me and My Destiny

From the womb of my mother
    to the day of my birth,
my destiny was written and sealed.

And I was set on a path
    from which I could grow
until the day it could be fulfilled.

Me and my destiny
    are forever bound
and will endure the extent of time.

Though some will try to obtain
    that in life I have gained,
they can never take what's mine.

So all praise is due
    to the Most High God,
who has given all things life,

Who, in his infinite understanding,
    saw the end from the beginning
and prepared the sacrifice,

Who, in the counsel of himself,
    saw it pleasingly fit
that I should come to be

And no weapon formed
    or force known to man
could stop me and my destiny.

Uniquely worded by
Andre "Doc" Lawrence

It Has Been an Honor

Here's to the host of men
    with whom I have endured
along my journey's way,

Who are among the few
    that maintained their honor
and from the code didn't stray,

Who, when faced with the choice
    of saving themselves,
became the sacrifice instead,

Believing that before the day would come
    that he would trade in his soul,
he'd rather be cold and dead.

For he knows his position
    and will never waver,
and surely God will have his back.

And he will face the obstacles
    that are sure to come
with his manhood still intact.

It has been an honor and a privilege
    to dwell among you
and learn from you what I can.

So know with a certainty
    that I am your brother
and at your side I will always stand.

Our similar upbringing
    created a bond;
though not blood, it runs much deeper.

And no matter the course
    this life may take us,
I will remain my brother's keeper.

Uniquely worded by
Andre "Doc" Lawrence

Hear Ye, Hear Ye
(All You Battle-Ready Souls)

Hear ye, hear ye,
    all you battle-ready souls,
Who constantly roam
    those streets you patrol.
In constant search
    of something to fold
And to acquire such,
    your hearts turn cold.
And despite the cost,
    you will pursue
Without care or limit
    of what you will do.
For heartless and void
    you have become,
Because all the drugs and liquor
    has left you numb

To the point you're fading
    due to declining health,
And your man in the mirror
    doesn't recognize himself.
But for minimal profit,
    you continue a course,
Claiming countless lives
    with no remorse.
As if God himself
    has appointed thee
to inflict a reign of terror
    and misery.
Hear ye, hear ye,
    all you battle-ready souls,
Who descend from a people
    who were brought and sold
And became the foundation
    upon which this nation islaid
And had to fight and die
    to become more than slaves.
Defying tumultuous odds
    and the American dream campaign,
Having lost their identity, culture,
    and God-given name,

Andre Lawrence

They persevered with hopes
    of what would one day be,
That the generations to come
    would be utterly free.
So hear ye, hear ye,
    all you battle-ready souls,
With your broken dreams
    and unaccomplished goals,
Who shamelessly wage war
    upon yourselves in the streets
Because you don't know your worth
    or who you are meant to be,
Because a drug-induced state
    has become your constant norm,
Leaving you blind to the enemy
    and the weapons formed.
For there is war upon us,

one we can't avoid,
And they have deployed their agents
    that we may be destroyed.
So, all my battle-ready souls,
    who have been bred for war
And in constant search
    for something more,
Pick up thyself
    and clear thy mind
That your vision is sure
    and you will see the sign.
And let nothing hinder you
    or alter your sight,
For war has been waged against us;
    now it's time we fight.

Uniquely worded by
Andre "Doc" Lawrence

Cannibal Mentality

It is beyond reproach
    the illicit acts
and mentality of a selected few

Who senselessly kill
    for the sport of the thrill
then Facebook it for you to view.

Shameless and bold,
    they continue their course
with wings of pride at their back,

Playing god among men
    with each life they take,
but with no moral code intact.

So the mourning ensues
    as the rivers of blood
run a course throughout our homes

And all remnants of life
    are slowly consumed
until the day it is utterly gone.

But this art not be so
    for those who know
but have taken a silent stance.

Instead of turning the cheek
    and silently accepting defeat,
try standing and do what you can.

Bear no concerns for this life
    or that to be gained
because we're all subjected to sudden death.

And there will be no profits to gain
    or livelihoods to maintain
until that mentality is put in check!

Uniquely worded by
Andre "Doc" Lawrence

Sign of the Times

We're living in a strange new day
    filled with moral decay
and a society that's consumed by fear.

Imminent threats are on the rise,
    while nations create divides
as if the end of days is near.

With a constant increase in crime
    and the death toll at a constant climb,
some may view it safer to never leave their home.

But how much safer can that be
    with all the warring in the streets
and communities being turned into battle zones?

So in this desperate state
    subjected to a devastating fate,
from where does our hope derive?

There's no trust in our leaders
    for they only mislead us
and are constantly in disguise.

For most are pawns in a role
    subjected to someone else's control
and are powerless to implement
any change.

And with their false presence of strength,
    they deceive us without consent,
so our position here remains the same.

So for any semblance of hope
    to take root in this equation
and so our world doesn't come to a
drastic end,

We need sincere leaders of the people
    who will build up relations
and a world that we can all live
herein.

Uniquely worded by
Andre "Doc" Lawrence

All that My Eyes Have Seen

No one knows
     all that my eyes have seen
Or the amount I've suffered
     since my early teens,

Born into a world
     that shatters dreams,
And most do survive
     by any means

Where the streets are filled
     with hypes and fiends,
Who, for the fix of the day,
     do abominable things,

Where death is consistent
     so there are constant screams
And ambulance pickups
     are a normal scene.

No one knows
    all that my eyes have seen
Or the horrors that haunt me,
    my nightmares bring.

No one knows
    all that my eyes have seen
Or the hours on life's clock
    that are left for me.

So judge me not
    no matter how things may seem,
Because no one knows
    all that my eyes have seen.

Uniquely worded by
Andre "Doc" Lawrence

Real Nigga Rich

Born in at the bottom
    with the lowly outcast,
suffering from constant lack,

Motivated by your ambitions,
    you make life-changing decisions
in pursuit of the paper stack.

For the CREAM
    (Cash Rules Everything Around Me),
you're going all in.

You're up early making moves,
    chasing this dream,
as you advance toward your expected end.

And with time, you begin to rise,
    becoming the light of everyone's eyes,
as you bathe in your small success.

But the goons are on the prowl,
    on the hunt for you and your lifestyle,
and it's yo head they want on the platter next.

They say money equals power
    and brings a whole lot of problems
and, in the end, you find life's a bitch.

But it was you who chose
    to set your sights on such goals;
that would only leave you real nigga rich.

Uniquely worded by
Andre "Doc" Lawrence

Bully Me Not

Is it my look
    or shade of skin
That ignites the evil
    that lies within?

For without cause,
    you invoked your will
And brought about a pain
    I was sure to feel.

With such harsh words,
    you taunted me so,
Leaving me feeling helpless
    and nowhere to go.

Quite often I wondered,
    what role did I play
At causing you the need
    to treat me this way?

Could it be my size
 or fashion sense
That causes you to act
 with such carelessness?

Could it be my lack
 of physical display,
Or are you upset at the fact
 that I'm openly gay?

Whatever the case,
 please end your plot,
And from this day forward,
 bully me not.

Uniquely worded by
Andre "Doc" Lawrence

The Letter

My people, I write this letter to you
    concerning the changing times,
that if we are to grow and become strong as a people,
    only in unity are we to shine.

I know it seems rough,
    but look at our past;
we've made it through all the pains.

We survived the long trips
    of being packed on slave ships
and endured the whips and chains.

But not only that;
    we've overcomeloss
of our culture and way of life,

Survived in a foreign land,
    fought and died to make a stand,
and we honor our heroes who paid the price.

So wake up, wake up,
    wake up, my people,
because it seems we've lost our way.

With the constant rise in violence
    and our leaders toned to silence,
is there no one who can lead us today?

Sadly, by far,
    it's been too long a struggle,
because by now, we should be ahead.

But for that to come true,
    we must all see it through,
because they would rather see us struggle until we're dead.

This letter was written
    to inspire my people,
to take a stand and unite as one.

And if not now
    while the clock's still running,
when will we ever get this job done?

Uniquely worded by
Andre "Doc" Lawrence

We Interrupt the Regularly Scheduled Program

We interrupt the regularly scheduled program
    to bring you an up-to-the-minute beat.

It appears our children have been targeted
    all across this nation
as their bodies pile up in the streets.

We interrupt the regularly scheduled program
    to shed light on the changing times.

Is it not those who have sworn to protect
    delivering sudden death
as if it were a victimless crime?

We interrupt the regularly scheduled program
    to say that which must be said:

Public relations are on the fall
    while gun violence rises tall,
leaving countless innocent dead.

We interrupt the regularly scheduled program
    to have a moment to pause and reflect.

Let the lives that were lost
    inspire a brighter future
and this we never forget.

We interrupt the regularly scheduled program
    to be the voice of reconciliation and love,

To bring calm to the streets
    and the raging beast
and stop the rivers of blood.

We interrupt the regularly scheduled program . . .

Uniquely worded by
Andre "Doc" Lawrence

In the Wake of Summer

In the wake of summer,
    trees have budded, flowers have bloomed,
and the grass is fertile green.

The sun sits high
    in an open sky
and shines on everything.

In the wake of summer,
    the kids are out and roam about
as school comes to a season's end.

The block is packed,
    and everyone awaits the night
for the party that's sure to begin.

In the wake of summer,
    in its darkest hour,
death will surely strike.

And no budding flowers
    or plans of partying
will prevent this taking of life.

In the wake of summer

Uniquely worded by
Andre "Doc" Lawrence

American-Less

They say as an American,
    one has inalienable rights
and the freedom to pursue one's dreams.

Yet I have been branded an American
    but am of African descent,
so the concept takes on a different means,

Unlike my white counterparts
    who have established this creed
and a constitution to reflect its intent.

And if this constitution
    stands as the law of the land,
then of man, I am only a percent.

Some say America is the land of the free
    and home of the brave
and the pursuit of happiness is for all to have.

But I have been deemed an American,
    and such a pursuit
has never been within my grasp.

One could question this logic,
    but history bears an account
of the cruelty at America's hand,

Of how they feed the native's disease
    and hung me from trees,
and I am to believe I'm American.

I guess you would have me
    recite your anthems and salute your flag
as if all is well and fine

And the crimes you've committed
    to establish this nation
we'll ignore and pay no mind.

So I conclude, American I'm not
    for obvious reasons,
and the truth I am not blind from seeing.

And I propose this question,
    Does not being an American
make me less of a human being?

Uniquely worded by
Andre "Doc" Lawrence

Social Address

It appears
    we find ourselves
at that sad place in time

Where we must again
    address the issue
of our racial divide.

No longer can we
    remain silent
or pretend to be color-blind

Or falsely believe justice
    will come
in due time.

For it is evident
    by their actions
there's no shame in their crime,

How they will
    senselessly take life
and pay it no mind.

Though protest
    is on the rise
and tension on high

And marches
    have become the norm,
while officials tell lies.

It's a tragedy
    but truth
and wears no disguise

That the police
    are the culprits
who have taken these lives.

So the whole nation
    became shocked
and totally surprised

When violence
    returned back
from whence it reside.

You created the circumstances
    that provoked
all that has transpired.

You invoked force
    when a little love
was all that was required.

Uniquely worded by
Andre "Doc" Lawrence

I Have a Clear View through My Window

I have a clear view through my window
    to the main line of the darkest streets,
And upon this line, there is endless crime
    for it is the place the darkest souls seek.

I have a clear view through my window
    to the sadness of broken homes,
Where the children are afraid to play and Daddy's far away,
    leaving Mother to raise the children alone.

I have a clear view through my window
    to the women who move in square;
Though most come and go, be it rain, sleet, or snow,
    someone's bound to be roaming there.

I have a clear view through my window
    where violence consumes the land
And all the young boys carry guns for toys
    and kill whomever they can.

I have a clear view through my window
    to the world that before me lies,
And even in its damaged state, I still have faith
    that a change will come in time.

I have a clear view through my window . . .

Uniquely worded by
Andre "Doc" Lawrence

I Wonder, Will They Listen?

I wonder, Will they listen
    if I ask them to take a view
Of the world today in which we live,
    would they even have a clue?

I wonder, Will they listen
    if I spoke in an aggressive tone,
Saying, "Change your ways to ensure better days,"
    or would they continue to carry on?

I wonder, Will they listen
    if I shouted with all my might
To open their eyes and realize
    that there's a real purpose to life?

I wonder, Will they listen
    if I begged, on bended knee,
To look around and see how lives are being torn down,
    would this not be clear to see?

I wonder, Will they listen
    or fail to interpret the truth,
That the path we lay and what we display
    ultimately affect our youth?

I wonder, Will they listen
    before they experience a fall,
Because in life lived fast, nothing truly lasts
    and, in the end, you lose it all?
I wonder, Will they listen
    and give thought to the words I preach?
Or has life today led so many astray
    that all are beyond my reach?

I wonder, Will they listen,
    for what I present is a message of light?
We've been in darkness too long, and how longer will we carry on
    before we decide to make things right?

Uniquely worded by
Andre "Doc" Lawrence

This Road

As I stroll along
    this concrete road,
Through the valley of death
    and forgotten souls,

I came to the place
    of the known unknown,
Where the lifeless dwelled
    and freely roamed,

Where love and compassion
    have no place,
For violence and evil
    are its constant state,

Where on a daily basis,
    all life is drained
And patiently waits
    for its next life to claim.

So sad but true
    this road I've strolled,
And all that is,
    is dark and cold,

Where the sound of cries
    goes unheard,
For those who hear
    utter not a word.

These words I've composed
    may sound strange,
But they are the truth in describing
    this dying age.

Uniquely worded by
Andre "Doc" Lawrence

Rizin' against the Oddss

I had to rize
    from beneath the concrete
to enduring constant storms.

I'm product of my environment,
    and life wasn't sweet,
and violence was the constant norm.

My world was more like a whirlwind,
    yet I didn't conform,
though chaos was at a steady pace.

Yet with these odds against me,
    I stayed focused on my mission
with a never-yielding faith.

So in my pursuit of happiness,
    to acquire a better life,
I'm resilient at every turn.

And my determination
    and self-motivation
bear witness to the lessons I've learned.

See, though I come from the ghetto
    and a harsh upbringing,
that doesn't define the whole sum of me.

And I am living proof
    that not odds nor from whence I came
could interfere with who I am meant to be.

Uniquely worded by
Andre "Doc" Lawrence

Tragic Reality

What a brave new day
    or, rather, moment in time
we find ourselves within,

Where newscasts blast
    and internet chatters
as the dawn of day begins.

And before the day is started,
    someone's dearly departed
and the losses are getting close to home.

And around noonday,
    another body is hauled away
another tragedy and victim unknown.

So as the sun begins to set,
    we watch, pray, and protect,
for we are aware of this painful truth

That we have reached a point in time
    where police commit the crime
of killing our unarmed youth.

Uniquely worded by
Andre "Doc" Lawrence

This Is My Pain Eulogized

They say in life,
    you will endure your share of pain,
but mine has been rather consistent.

It has become a present stay
    in my day-to-day,
a constant thorn in my existence.

And with each new day, dawn,
    a new pain comes;
the only difference is the form it takes.

And fight as I do,
    with hopes of making it through,
I'm overwhelmed with little escape.

For in the eyes of many,
    I am strength and hope for a new beginning,
a living truth for their eyes to see.

But most tend to love me
    for what they want me to be for them
and not for who I am meant to be.

With this revelation
    and understanding, no doubt,
my pain is multiplied tenfold.

I look out to the world,
    at all that's going on
and see how the hearts of the young have turned cold

And see how our seeds
    commit devious deeds
because they're blind and uninformed

And how they pursue this course
    with no remorse
and live it as the norm.

Andre Lawrence

Society will make claims
    but never take blame
for the role they undoubtedly played,

How they meticulously planned
    to destroy as best as they can
the descendants of those once enslaved.

For when slavery came to an end,
    segregation came in,
and America became black and white.

But whites held the reins of power,
    so they killed, raped, and devoured
every shred of black America's rights

And then put things in play
    that would leave blacks divided and in disarray
to support their perception and view

That blacks are just former slaves,
    subhumans to be encaged,
and 'til this day, this ideal stands true.

So maybe now the world will see
    what we have always known;
there is a reason for the tears in our eyes.

Now having said what I said,
    I hope you understand
this is my pain eulogized.

Uniquely worded by
Andre "Doc" Lawrence

The Incline of Injustice

Sadly, there seems
    to be no decline
or suppression in the onslaught attacks.

It's evident the police
    have made up their minds
to continue their campaign of murdering blacks.

There's no coincidence
    for each incident
conclusion looks quite the same.

A routine situation
    leads to loss of life,
and an officer is the blame.

Yet in the same breath,
    they say we should offer respect
to those who serve and protect.

But how can this be
    with their continued killing spree
and their actions showing no regret?

I'd like nothing more
    than to fully support
those who wear the shield,

For there is much to be said
    for those who brave the battle
and risk their lives every day in the field.

But inside this developing pattern
    of deadly, unprovoked action
by the company of men in blue,

You have forced my decision,
    leaving me in a position
where I can no longer invest trust in you.

Uniquely worded by
Andre "Doc" Lawrence

Rivers of Blood

Rivers of blood
    run a constant course
throughout the city I know as home,

Went from Chi-Town to Chi-Raq
    due to the violent impact,
and are truly a battle zone

Because on any given day,
    violence will erupt
and spark havoc throughout the streets,

And those in the game
    promote a death campaign
like wild and unruly beast.

Not once taking time
    to weigh in the cost
for the actions they do engage,

They senselessly kill,
    and more blood is spilled
in the heat of their burning rage.

So no corner is safe
    and no household immune
from the violence that has gripped our land.

And this course will remain
    and go unchanged
until someone takes a stand,

A true stand for change
    with a sincere devotion
to endure beyond the dawning sun,

Because anything less
    than our sincere, devoted best,
these rivers of blood will continue to run.

Uniquely worded by
Andre "Doc" Lawrence

These Are the Tears I Cry

It was in my early teens
    that I embraced the street scene
that these tears began to form.

And how often they did fall
    as I faced each tragic loss
while enduring this deadly storm.

Oh, how I'd like to deny
    those many nights I cried
as if crying was the norm.

But I can recall each death
    and see clearly the last breath
of those lives I constantly mourn.

Bang, bang, bang!
    rings the sound of the gun,
evidence of another life lost.

Now the streets just claimed two victims,
    one to the grave, the other to thesystem,
and what a hella price it cost.

And yet as time progressed,
    so did my tears,
as the death toll continues to rise.

Killing has become a sport,
    and the youth are the cohorts
who contribute to their own demise.

And sadly so,
    as my tears freely flow,
as I embrace this hardening truth

That with no leaders to lead,
    to help change this course,
I see no future for our youth,

Because it's not just the good
    or even the bad;
it's our young who's dying young.

And if I had the power
    to change this course,
I'd undo all that has been done.

But what I lack in power,
    I'll make up in will,
because for change, I'll sincerely try.

But until that day comes,
    when peace rises like the sun,
these are the tears I cry.

                                      Uniquely worded by
                                    Andre "Doc" Lawrence

Bad Times upon Us

If you pause for a second
    and take in the view
of what has become the norm,

You'd have to admit
    it's conflict consumed
like a constant raging storm.

Death is the capital
    that backs the dollar,
and the cost is human lives.

And those in power
    willing set upon a course
that will bring about our demise.

As if they can't see the impact
    of such irrational reactions
and the devastation it will bring,

We're already a nation
    where countless suffer;
they're too impoverished to even dream.

The fatality rate
    is at a constant climb
and on course to reach its peak

And will set breaking records
    with willing help
of those who roam the streets.

For void of conscious
    and moral code,
they embrace the reaper's way.

To be present in life,
    death shall follow,
so they kill from day to day.

In this state of mind,
    they're utterly blind,
and none are truly safe,

Forcing those who can
    to uproot their lives
with hopes of some escape.

Sadly, it has become evident
    that bad times are no longer coming;
they are here in living color.

And this reality should be enough
    to remove our petty differences
that we begin to love one another.

                    Uniquely worded by
                  Andre "Doc" Lawrence

Ye though I Walk

Ye though I walk
through the valley
of the shadow of death,
I shall fear no evil.

For when I got down
to the valley,
I quickly realized
it was just me and my people.

Trapped in an ever
constant state of depression,
so pay attention y'all
because class is now in session.

At this revelation,
my body became
tensed and chilled.

So I began a closer observation
that I would recognize the illusion
from what was real.

Not wanting to bear false witness,
I kept my focus,
and after witnessing
one too many scenes,
I realized
this was the valley of the hopeless.

Though death was ever present,
it played the shadows well,
for there was no need to rush
to claim the souls
that were already living in hell.

And hell it is,
or at least
to a certain degree.

Andre Lawrence

See, here we are,
the perpetrator and the victim,
contributing to our own misery.

For our condition here
is all on us
and continues due to
lack of leaders,
lack of love,
and lack of trust.

See, these three things
in nation building are essential
to our development and improving.

And certainly, without them,
we'll all bear witness
of becoming a nation to lie in ruins.

So to my former street bosses
who overcame, though suffered losses,
but have fallen silent,
living quiet on the other side,
believing it to be better,

I strongly encourage you
to reassume your role
as boss and take control,
because the status of our situation
is critical,
and the time is now or never.

Uniquely worded by
Andre "Doc" Lawrence

America's Outcast

I'm the sleeping lion
    filled with silent rage
that's been hunted and trapped like game.

I've been stripped of humanity
    and given a number
in place of my God-given name,

Met with extreme force
    in the form of judicial recourse
under the pretense of justice served,

Charged with a criminal act
    that's an even bigger crime to enforce,
so pay attention to these spoken words.

Rise and shine,
    my fellow man,
well, those of you who can.

See, though the sun sits high
    and brightly shines,
it's still dark in this abominable land.

I done walked the four corners
    of this world I'm in,
running from sin to sin.

And be it not for my faith
    and all I hold true,
I would've thrown the towel in.

I've suffered loss and endured
    like the many around me
and maintain from year to year.

And when contact is made
    by the family away,
I'm forced to reflect hope from here.

I'm often associated
    as the lost and forgotten,
he that is no more.

If you haven't figured out who I am,
    I'm America's outcast
inmate number 20739-424.

Uniquely worded by
Andre "Doc" Lawrence

They Say that I Am a Racist

"They say that I am a racist"

But who traveled across the seas
    and committed human robbery
with purpose and a devious plan,

And those who survived the trip
    were chained, raped, and whipped
and treated as the lesser man.

"They say that I am a racist"

Because I refuse to be silent
    to this nation's vicious history of violence
or surrender my destiny.

"They say that I am a racist"

But who's been enslaved
    and sent to an early grave
and often found hanging from a tree.

"They say that I am a racist"

Simply because I hold my head up high
    and promote black pride
to inspire hope for the generations to come.

"They say that I am a racist"

But do not history bear witness
    to all atrocities
and by whose hand it was done.

"They say that I am a racist"

Because I won't live a lie
    and turn a blind eye
to the reality I often see.

And from our first encounter
    up until this present day,
it has been you who has been attacking me.

"But they say that I am a racist."

Uniquely worded by
Andre "Doc" Lawrence

US Occupation

If you watch the news
    or listen to the radio station,
you can't help but feel
    we're in a crisis situation.

For they are streaming it live
    with no filtration:
unarmed blacks murdered by cops
    all across the nation.

Videos show
    how, with no hesitation,
they resort to extreme force
    with no justification.

I know the truth
    they miss the days
when we were on the plantation,

When they could
    buy, sell, and kill us
with no explanation.

So now we gather
    and march
to vent our frustrations,

Demanding justice
    from the system
and passing due reparations.

All the while,
    we're still dying,
and that's a harsh revelation,

Because if they're not
    killing us in the street,
we're subjected to mass incarceration.

I just call it
    how I see it
with no exaggeration.

What I beheld
    is an institution
hell-bent on my annihilation.

Some will doubt
    but this truth
with no speculation.

And it's the reality
    we now live
under US occupation.

Uniquely worded by
Andre "Doc" Lawrence

The Cruel Truth

With cruel intentions,
    they weaponized religion,
and their mission had no pure intent.

Yet 'til this day,
    we still gather and pray,
extending our silent consent.

For the injustice we suffer
    has not gone unnoticed,
but it's on us to make the demand.

But we're caught up in fights
    about who's God or who's right;
we lose sight of the fight at hand.

And in our lack of vision
    to truly understand our condition,
we've become puritans in a damaging way.

We've assimilated our captors
    and taken on the culture
of the very ones who made us slaves.

How sad this sounds
    but so true indeed
and remains evident by this simple fact.

For the something that is nothing,
    we will destroy one another,
and in truth, there is no denying that.

Now as you part with these words
    and whatever effect they may have had,
I encourage you to find your truth.

And as time marches on,
    establish new norms,
ones that will uplift you.

Uniquely worded by
Andre "Doc" Lawrence

Today We Gather

Today we gather
    to pay honor to those
who bravely set the tone,

Who, when no one else
    would be that example,
became our cornerstone,

Who, in trying times,
    never wavered
but proudly embraced the fight,

Who spoke with volume
    and never cowered
quietly in the night,

Who, when faced with the choice
    to live free or die,
accepted the consequences of their acts

And, having made their choice,
    pursued their course
without ever looking back.

Today we gather
    to pay honor to those
whose life's work offers us direction.

And the trails they blazed
    shall be our constant reminder
and a continual living testament.

Today we gather
    and honorthose
to whom there are no equals.

They've sacrificed
    and given life
for the betterment of our people.

So let's lift them up
    and honor them so
as if nothing else even matters.

And let us never forget
    as time marches on
that this is why we gather.

Uniquely worded by
Andre "Doc" Lawrence

History's Present

Where do I even begin to write
    these words I want to say,
that could express the fullness of my feelings
    on how I feel today?

And knowing that
    every day that goes by,
there's sure to come some change,

But not in the case
    concerning my people,
and I find that oddly strange.

Why do my people
    often fall victim
and feel doomed to a certain degree?

Was not the law of the land
    installed for all men,
or did it exclude you and me?

For how can it be
    that through all these years,
our position here seems the same?

Was not the sacrifice made
    and our debt to society paid,
or did our heroes all die in vain?

And to look at today,
    it resembles yesterday,
but it's being played on different grounds.

Instead of the plantation and a noose,
    we're incarcerated in groups;
can you relate to how sad that sounds?

Do we not remember the struggles,
    the lives that were lost,
the torturing of whips and chains?

We only fight for our rights
    that in equality, we might
have a chance to truly gain.

Malcolm, Martin, Medgar, and Harriet—
    in those names we held our trust;
they paved the way
    for the present day,
but the future is up to us.

Let us become one
    or dig ourgraves;
let us unite as apeople
    or as modern-day slaves.

                                Uniquely worded by
                            Andre "Doc" Lawrence

Am I Not Worthy?

Am I not worthy
    of a chance at life
to fulfill my hopes and dreams

And the freedom to pursue
    without pressing odds
no matter how strange they seem?

Am I not worthy
    of inalienable rights
in the fullness of God's intent,

That the man in me
    can freely be
without legislative consent?

Am I not worthy
    to love and be loved
and, against the odds, decide my fate,

Without constantly being judged
    and forced to stand trial
before those who will discriminate?

Am I not worthy
    to live in a world
where I'm not viewed as the constant threat

And my life,
    just as all lives matter,
is regarded with respect?

Am I not worthy,
    like all human beings,
to a life I don't have to defend

And not put to shame
    for whence I came
or the color of my skin?

    Am I not worthy?

Uniquely worded by
Andre "Doc" Lawrence

New Thought, New Man

It has been said "So as a man thinketh, so is he."

But as a young embryo
    in the safe confines of my mother's womb,
my only thoughts were to be.

And at the age of five or six
    when I could read and write,
my level of thinking reached newer heights.

See, I started to dream and imagine things,
    mostly due to the books I read
and the things I've seen.

It's been said "So as a man thinketh, so is he."

And dreaming is the evidence
    that the mind never sleeps.

At around twelve or thirteen, I began to entertain new thoughts—
    no, not new in the sense of new in thinking, but in doing.

But because there was no thought,
    I eventually got lost
down the road I was pursuing.

    Again, it's been said, "So as a man thinketh, so is he."

And my reward for the goals
    down the road I chose
left me void and empty.

Now from my early twenties
    to the present day,
I've grown a lot
    and in many ways.

Andre Lawrence

I now consider the cause and effect
    of the things I think
and weigh the total cost.

I don't rush to react
    or verbally attack;
I simply embrace a new thought.

This is the mental level
    we all must reach
if throughout time we are to stand,

Because every positive new thought
    is a building block
in creating a new man.

And just like I mentioned time and time again,

"So as a man thinketh, so is he."

And I pray the new thoughts
    I've chosen to embrace
will ultimately be what defines me.

Uniquely worded by
Andre "Doc" Lawrence

I Am a ~~Human~~ Being

Society at large
    has bestowed upon
every title but my own

And, with tireless effort,
    maintained resistance
that the truth may never be known.

For at every turn
    throughout the course of time,
when truth would rear its face,

The ruling powers in play
    exhausted all measures
to ensure truth would not see the light of day.

So as time reeled on
    and truth restrained
and hidden in an unmarked grave,

That when the question arise,
    does here stand a man?
I was awarded the title of slave.

Slavery ran its course
    or taken another form
and was to be abolished throughout the land.

And war was fought
    for equalities cost,
yet I'm decreed three-fifths of man.

I've been savagely handled
    and wrongfully dealt
at the discretion of the oppressor's hand.

I've been Negro, Afro,
    and commonly black
and now African American.

These bestowed-upon titles
    are simply titles,
and none of these I claim.

Neither Negro, Afro,
    or African American
validates the origin from whence I came.

I am the promise of the future
    though I've been robbed of my past;
bestow upon me what you like,
    but I'll always be a human being first and last.

Uniquely worded by
Andre "Doc" Lawrence

The Day Freedom Came

The day freedom came,
    I was adorned in shackles and chains
And put on display like a human castaway
    at the human stock exchange

Where I was to be sold for a bid
    at the highest price
And fieldwork would become the chore
    I would endure for life.

The day freedom came,
    I was out tilling the land,
Working long days and nights
    at Master's command.

See, the plantation was home,
    and a bed of straw is for sleep.
Master had one rule that governed all:
    "you don't work, you don't eat."

The day freedom came,
    I was on the underground;
I heard north is where a man is free,
    so I was headed northbound.

Change is on the rise
    as North and South engage in war,
And if the North claims the victory,
    there will be slavery no more.

The day freedom came,
    in some places,
A slave was still a slave.

The word hadn't reached
    those parts yet,
That they were free to choose their own way.

The day freedom came,
    it was greeted with a sigh of relief
Then a burst of cheer,

Because as a people, we've prayed
    for this coming day,
And now it's finally here.

Uniquely worded by
Andre "Doc" Lawrence

Justice or Else

We, the people
    who have suffered and died,
given countless lives
    in the quest to be rendered free,

Stand today one as a whole,
    fearless and bold,
for all the world to see.

We, the people
    who bear the scars
and ill remarks
    of racism at its best,

Know now our path
    and valued worth
and will never settle for less.

We, the people
    being once the victim,
shall become the victor
    and will fight until our last breath

And will not retreat
    or surrender
even in the face of death.

We, the people
    whose voices go unheard
by those in congressional seats,

Who willingly remain silent
    and turn a blind eye
while our children savagely die in the streets,

We, the people
    having endured your worst,
embark on a mission
    bigger than one's self,

Because as I've stated,
    we are the people,
and today it's justice or else!

Uniquely worded by
Andre "Doc" Lawrence

I Am the Undesirable — Part 1

From my conception at birth,
    my worth was assessed,
and boundaries were set in place.

And social norms were erect
    to bear the effect
that I would remain lost and without a trace.

I have been shipped and caged
    with the destiny to be enslaved
in the name of capital gain.

With no culture intact
    to keep me spiritually rooted,
my prayers went in vain.

See, in the land of my captors,
    I've become suitably fit
to be oppressed by any means.

In their eyes, I'm chattel,
    something less than human,
a most undesirable thing.

And history bears witness
    to the truth of their crimes,
and their legislation supports the act.

I've been beaten, raped,
    and killed at random
simply for being black.

    I am the undesirable . . .

Uniquely worded by
Andre "Doc" Lawrence

I Am the Undesirable — Part 2

I am the economic prey
    that has sustained this nation
from its infancy to this present day.

I am the stolen goods harbored
    in the belly of the ship
who became the hell-bent runaway.

I am the just cause
    for laws to be enacted
to deprive me of inalienable rights.

I am the rebel on the rise
    who will not compromise,
and for freedom, I will continually fight.

I am the target of a nation
    who seeks only my demise
in every way and form.

They started out with slavery;
    now mass incarceration
has become their daily norm.

The truth is often seen,
    rarely heard,
so this truth is undeniable.

I'm viewed as filth,
    the scum of the earth;
I am the undesirable.

Uniquely worded by
Andre "Doc" Lawrence

I Am

I am he who comes
    and quiets the storm
That prevents total chaos
    from becoming the norm.

I am the adopted son
    to every mother I know
And sound voice of reason
    everywhere I go.

I am the strong black male
    who rose from the streets,
Bearing the scars of war,
    but never suffered defeat.

I am the lover to the women
    who shared my soul,
The sacred place of secrets
    that remain untold.

I am the breath of fresh air
    when it's hard to breathe,
The friend who will endure
    and never leave.

I am the centerpiece to the puzzle
    that puts it all sync,
The man with the mind
    causing you to pause and think.

I am son, I am brother,
    I am father, I am lover,
I am teacher, I am friend.

But truthfully, in the end,
    I am me,
And all these things are a part of
    who I am.

Uniquely worded by
Andre "Doc" Lawrence

The Darkness in which I Dwell

Through tears of pain,
    my anger is enflamed
as I become emotionally unattached.

I'm slowly consumed
    into the darkness that looms
as I continually fade to black.

Yet in the shadow of darkness,
    I am not afraid,
for there is no sense of fear.

It's as if the darkness
    has become my own,
and I am truly at home here.

With consuming thoughts
    in this perpetual state,
I pause to consider my fate,

Only to realize the sum
    from which I come
is a world where death awaits.

Having endured my fill
    of sorrow and pain,
for my heart has become a weeping well,

I retreat into the shadows
    and take refuge in the darkness,
where my soul has come to dwell.

Uniquely worded by
Andre "Doc" Lawrence

Strong Black Soul

I was stored in the loins
    of my great ancestors,
sealed 'til my time to be,

As they were cattled to a land
    through the adventurous route
on the backs of the waves of the sea.

Hard labor was the reward
    my forefathers were giving
and discipline for reproof.

And pain was ingrained
    down to the bone,
and my DNA bears this truth.

The rainy seasons lasted
    from generation to generation
without sunshine at all in sight.

But as they endured their hardships,
    they looked to the future,
to the day of the dawning light.

So much was designed
    to bring about my demise,
but yet I still exist,

I am the strong black soul
    of whom history bears an account
and never will forget.

Uniquely worded by
Andre "Doc" Lawrence

I Am Powerful

I am powerful
    though I descend
from the womb of the former slaves.

I am one of many
    who have suffered as such
among society's castaways.

I am powerful;
    though my road has been rough,
I press on toward brighter days.

I am the dark, lost soul
    that's been brought and sold
and abused in many ways.

I am powerful
    though some will see me for what they want
and not all that I can be.

They'll see the color of my skin,
    the relationship I'm in
without once ever seeing me.

Yet throughout my trials,
    hardships and woes,
and all I've had to face,

I know now with a certainty,
    though trials may come,
I will endure and never break.

I am powerful,
    and this exceeds what some may see
of my physical display.

And all the gifts
    that God has given me
can never be taken away.

    I am powerful!

Uniquely worded by
Andre "Doc" Lawrence

A Man Trying to Get Right with God

As I kneel today
    before your throne of grace
a broken shell of a man,

I pray that thou
    will hear my cry
and receive me into thy hands.

For like the king of fools,
    I ran through life
with my knowledge of a small degree,

Assuming all credit
    when it was you who protected me
from the dangers I couldn't foresee.

Having been born into a world
    where chance and circumstance
run a never-ending course

And the meek in the streets
    are viewed as weak
and the strong kill for sport,

With those limited options,
    a choice must be made,
whether it be right or wrong.

And I knew my choice
    would become my life,
and I would endure it on my own.

Like the prodigal son,
    leaning on my own understanding,
I journeyed through the valleys unknown,

Only to find myself
    lost and afraid
and a long way from home.

Moving forward with my life
    and those choices made,
I learned swiftly life was cold.

And with ego and pride
    being my guide,
I was left with a restless soul.

Having successfully endured
    and overcome these trials,
I'm on the path to a brand-new start.

And though I've been a fool
    and many other things,
today, I'm a man trying to get right with God.

Uniquely worded by
Andre "Doc" Lawrence

The Vowing Man

They say when a man
    has found his wife,
he has found a beautiful thing

And there's nothing else known
    in this world and beyond
that compares to the joy she brings.

For she is the embodiment of love
    and shelter of life
and wears devotion as a garment of praise

And she won't crack under pressure
    no matter how life tests her
and will be a comfort in those long, hard days.

Her inner strength
    is just like her beauty
beyond what the eyes can see.

And it's not just a blessing
    to be in her presence;
it's where I'm meant to be.

So before man and God,
    I make this vow;
to you I join my soul.

And we shall walk through life
    as husband and wife
and to love as our common goal.

Uniquely worded by
Andre "Doc" Lawrence

Atonement

Atonement can be defined
    as a journey
by which one travels to make amends,

For through this journey,
    one will make choices
that will determine if the means justify the ends.

Every man and woman
    will bear the burden
for the choices they have made.

And time will reveal
    and bear an account
of the character that has been displayed.

On average, as humans,
    we move through life
with our ambitions and nothing more,

Unaware of the fact
    of whom we offended
and what we should be atoning for.

An evaluation of self
    is where one must start
for the process to be bound in truth.

And as you atone for each wrong,
    you become confident and strong
and, in life, become living proof.

That atoning is not
    just consciously healthy
with benefits of keeping you whole.

It serves a purpose
    of far greater importance;
atonement cleanses the soul.

Uniquely worded by
Andre "Doc" Lawrence

From the Sidelines

From the sidelines, we're afforded
    only a limited view
of what appears to be.

And if we're quick to judge,
    we'll make the mistake of assuming
and bear witness to what our eyes didn't see.

From the sidelines, we hear
    but not fully understand
the full exchange of words being told.

So before we jump to conclusions
    and our mind fill with illusions,
let's wait 'til the story unfolds.

From the sidelines, our depiction
    is only a blur
filled with half-truths of our interpretation.

So it's best we remain silent
    and not offer our opinion
and do more harm to someone's situation.

Uniquely worded by
Andre "Doc" Lawrence

The Will of Concepts

Here I stand a man
    with only my hopes and dreams,
with the will to pursue
    and desire to fulfill;
I will accomplish them by any means.

Understanding this world
    and its views
of who I'm supposed to be,

I declared in my heart
    that a change must come,
and if need, he shall come through me.

I no longer accept
    the flawed concepts
that I've learned to keep me blind,

Passed on from generation
    to generation
with intent to restrict my mind.

One could point the finger
    and argue for days
about who's right or wrong.

But it's been our fears
    and the things we were taught
that kept us at odds this long.

So to this I say,
    let's do away
with the hate and the views that follow.

And let's learn to live
    and love today
and pursue those better tomorrows.

Uniquely worded by
Andre "Doc" Lawrence

Time, the Revealer

Time has a way
    of revealing things
the heart has always hidden.

And most will run through life\
    in constant search
of that one thing that is forbidden.

Without fully being aware,
    they blindly pursue
the direction of their heart,

With no concern or care
    of what their actions cost
and what may be torn apart.

It's been often said
    what we art not have
is what we desire most.

And true as that may be,
    we continue on
with hopes of gettingclose.

Though close in proximity,
    it remains just out of reach
and is the tormentor of your soul.

And the hopes of having it
    leaves you flying high,
but the reality is bitter cold.

There are no secrets to time
    for in it,
all is surely known,

Those private exchanges
    between lovers and friends
and even those moments when you're alone.

Uniquely worded by
Andre "Doc" Lawrence

Belizean Queen

Our first encounter
    is likened to a great escape,
and I'm the fill-in date,

For neither of us knew
    the encounter was destined
and would ultimately seal our fate,

Because in a short time span,
    after our dinner shared,
our paths would cross again.

We were reintroduced
    by Cheba, no doubt,
then the tale of us begin.

You were hesitant yet bold
    as you pursued your course
of claiming the prize of me.

You willingly gave me your heart
    and confessed your desires
of all you wanted to be.

Our connection was instant,
    and our chemistry, amazing,
forging a bond that's loyal and true.

And my body still tingles
    when I recall the feeling
of the warmth inside of you.

You are my Belizean queen
    who shook my world,
and against the odds you will never fold.

You came into my life
    and made it your home
and offered me a piece of your soul.

So now grateful am I,
    for in you, I have found
a treasure that all man seeks.

And there's no coincidence to this;
    what we have is meant,
and you are my destiny.

Uniquely worded by
Andre "Doc" Lawrence

Forever My White Girl

It's been an eternity of long days
    and endless nights
since our worlds were torn apart.

And in that lapse of time,
    you were never far from my mind
and always in my heart.

To say that I love you
    is an understatement,
for no words embody the truth.

And there has to be something
    far greater than love
to describe how I feel for you.

For if time is a testament
    to how what I feel endures
despite the seasons that change,

Know regardless of the course,
    our lives have taken
what I feel remains the same.

Though we were both young at heart
    when our worlds embraced,
we built a bond that most would envy.

And it didn't matter how far;
    when you called, I'd respond
and would come running whenever you'd need me.

From the outside looking in,
    some may draw the conclusion
that I'm sure was far from the truth.

They may have given me credit
    for upping your status,
but I was blessed by the presence of you.

Now I bear no illusions;
    the picture is perfectly clear:
you're a wife in a brand-new world.

Just know that part of me
    is forever yours
and you'll always be my white girl.

Uniquely worded by
Andre "Doc" Lawrence

Sue Mama

Shame on time
    for being so cruel
and keeping our worlds apart.

Though it seems a lifetime
    since last I've seen you,
you were always near to my heart.

Though no verbal words
    have been exchanged,
we communicate through simple text.

The anticipation runs high,
    causing my mind
to travel back in time to reflect.

You were the unplucked rose
    so sweet and gentle,
and I was the unworthy fool,

For I couldn't comprehend
    how one such as yourself
would give me the greatest part of you.

And being the fool that I was,
    I became lost and confused,
lacking the wisdom of what to do.

And though I would suffer the remorse,
    I let fear run its course
and forfeited my precious treasure of you.

And I only ask now
    that you look through the eyes
of a man who was once a fool.

And know that if I have,
    it was never my intent
to bring any form of harm to you.

Now moving right along
    to the present day,
having established this reconnect,

I see you've moved on in ways
    and your last name has changed,
which all I do respect.

So I ask for nothing,
    but I'll gratefully accept
what can be given without raising alarm,

Because I intend for my words
    to always ring true
and never to bring you harm.

Uniquely worded by
Andre "Doc" Lawrence

Pride of Tennessee

From the rising of the sun
    'til the day is done,
I condition myself for war,

Because I know my opponent
    awaits the moment
I'll show weakness out on the court.

So after the whistle blows,
    marking the start of the game,
I'm on alert as I play my role.

And I plat my position
    with acute precision
as I stay focused and in control.

On the battlefield of the court,
    in my warrior mode,
I'm scrappin' on every play,

Because losing is not an option
    no matter how good the game;
my team needs victory at the end of the day.

I am one of many
    who have journeyed this road
and took this game to another degree.

I fought bravely in battle
    and lived in the moment;
I am the pride of Tennessee!

Uniquely worded by
Andre "Doc" Lawrence

Here's to the Couple

Here's to the couple
    who have taken the vow
To endure in this life
    more than a country mile,

To persevere with patience
    and a love bond of truth
And freely live life fully
    as in the days of your youth,

To always communicate
    should uncertainty arise
And fight fiercely for love
    and not its demise.

Here's to the couple
    I pray will endure to the end,
And if not for their love,
    then for their love for me as a friend.

Uniquely worded by
Andre "Doc" Lawrence

Inspired by John

Tasha Brown

It's been a while now
    since our paths have crossed,
and not a word was ever spoken.

Life's circumstances
    set our worlds apart,
but the bond was never broken.

Some would call it chance,
    but I believe in destiny
because what will shall surely be.

Through the course of time,
    you have crossed my mind,
and it's evident you haven't forgotten about me.

So excited was I
    at the sound of your voice
during our conversation over the phone.

You were talking that talk
    and kept me smiling
while you made fun of my proper tone.

We both have grown
    with the passing of time,
a fact that remains to be true.

But no matter how much
    time should pass,
Tasha Brown, I'll never forget about you.

Uniquely worded by
Andre "Doc" Lawrence

Gratitude

In no particular order,
 you have, without question,
become a moving force.

You were the inspiration
 and motivation
that guided me along this course.

When I was in doubt,
 you were certain
that fulfillment was at hand.

So I stayed focused
 and prepared myself
that I might have a fighting chance.

It was your words of wisdom
    and constant counsel
that helped ensure victory would be won.

So I thank you dearly
    in the role you played
in the better man I have become.

Uniquely worded by
Andre "Doc" Lawrence

On this Day

On this day,
    all honor is due
to a woman who possesses style and grace,

Who endures each day
    despite the ups and downs
with a gentle, smiling face.

On this day,
    a celebration will commence,
and new memories you'll create to share.

And as time rolls by,
    you'll reflect on this day
and all who were present there.

On this day,
    it's all about you,
so feel free to do as you like.

But if nothing goes as planned,
    you live to try again,
and maybe next year, you'll get it right.

    Happy birthday.

Uniquely worded by
Andre "Doc" Lawrence

Farewell, Linde

Here's to that woman
    who has endured
efficiently with style and grace,

Who always made an effort
    to ensure the job was done
and did it all with a smiling face,

Who, on every encounter,
    had a warm greeting
and seemed bitter or down,

Who is of the few on the job
    you were glad to see coming
and happy to be around,

Who is full of laughs
    and bustin' dance moves in the hall
and has given more than she'll ever know.

Though we say farewell
    as your journey here ends,
it's bittersweet to have to see you go.

Uniquely worded by
Andre "Doc" Lawrence

Juneteenth

It was June 19,
    1865,
that this moment in history unfolds.

The civil war was done,
    and emancipation was won,
and our ancestors no longer could be sold.

So we humbly gather
    where honor is due
for those who have paved the way,

Whose sacrifice
    and constant fight
are the reason for our present day.

And for all that has been lost
    and what yet must be gained,
we hold this day as a mark in time,

That as we move forward
    toward our goal of recovery,
this struggle never leaves our mind,

That we may not unwittingly
    take for granted
the total sum of what's been paid,

For it was our mothers and fathers,
    sisters and brothers
forced into the role asslave.

So as we reflect on our past
    and address the present,
it's the future where the promise lies.

Though we've been held down
    for quite a while now,
it is time for us to rise.

Uniquely worded by
Andre "Doc" Lawrence

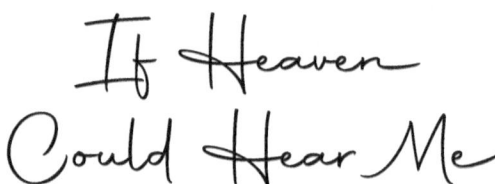

If Heaven Could Hear Me

Please allow me a moment
    to express in words
as only your father can.

And once all is said,
    I hope your love for me lives
and I'm not seen as a lesser man.

Along the way, things got crazy
    with me and your mom
and sometimes were even rough.

But the blame is all mine
    for the choices I made
and not being there enough.

But my lack of being present
    was never about you,
and there never was a lack of love.

I was just lost hurt and broken
    and searching for something,
so I surrendered myself to drugs.

Under constant influence
    in a world of my own,
what mattered was far from view.

I didn't give a damn about me,
    so I couldn't consider
how my actions were affecting you.

But it's quite evident though
    when we speak on the phone,
I hear the bitterness within your tone.

And my only response
    is "Calm down and listen,"
but like me, you're too headstrong.

Andre Lawrence

And I can't even be mad
    for in my absence, you thrived,
so know I am always proud.

You charted your own path
    and accomplished great things,
and never once have you let me down.

So looking toward the future
    and the promise that lies,
I pray for good times instead of the bad.

And I hope me and you
    can continue to build
the relationship we never had.

For in the end, my princess,
    you are my daughter,
that part of me that's always familiar.

And as your father,
    I love you always and forever,
Heaven Destiny Garcia.

Uniquely worded by
Andre "Doc" Lawrence

Here's to you,
the faithful andtrue,
Who have graciously given
what God has given to you.

Without doubt or concern,
you opened your heart,
Becoming witnesses that God's
love will never depart,

Bringing hope to the souls
behind the walls of stone
And the assurance in this life,
they're never alone.

For the Lord is the keeper
of all who believe,
And their constant companion
he'll always be.

But to you, the chosen
who have answered the call,
Who are battle-tested
and will never fall,

Who have endured your stripes
and carried your cross
With unshakable faith
when all seemed lost,

For the time and service
you gave without fee,
Knowing the blessings of the Lord
would be bestowed upon thee,

It gives me great honor
to proudly say
Thank you for Charis
and putting God's love on display.

Uniquely worded by
Andre "Doc" Lawrence

Kwanzaa

The first principle, Umoja,
    we define as "unity"
and must be maintained at whatever cost,

For to lose the unity
    of our family and community,
then as a people, we are truly lost.

Kujichagulia is the second principle,
    and "self-determination"
is how it is defined.

Becoming more self-aware
    we must take possession of our destiny
and set a standard that will transcend time.

"Collective work" and "responsibility"
    are what Ujima defines
and come third on our principle list.

And the failure to come together
    and work out all our problems,
those issues will only persist.

We integrate our resources
    to become economically sound
through the practice of the principle Ujamaa.

Nia represents purpose
    that all of us have,
and our creativity is reflected through Kuumba.

The last principle is Imani,
    and it represents our faith
that shall sustain us until the fight is won

And is the foundation
    upon which all principles lie
and shall endure those trials to come.

Kwanzaa is a collective
    of many principles
as means to a desired end,

That with constant practice,
    we would reconnect
to that place from where we begin.

In touch with our roots,
    that ancestral lineage,
our heritage is now intact.

We present ourselves whole
    to all of mankind
and take our legacy back.

Uniquely worded by
Andre "Doc" Lawrence

Farewell, FMC

It's been a long time coming,
    but we're finally here,
the day I say farewell

To a company of people
    who treated me kindly
and didn't make my life a living hell.

Through this awkward journey,
    respect was garnered
and reflected among us all.

We performed the task
    that was set before us,
whether it was big or small.

Even on those days
    that were a total drag
and someone was emotionally drained,

We'd find a way
    to pull through the day
so that person wouldn't go insane.

For most in this field,
    it's just a job
that they perform, and then they leave.

But for those of you
    I have come to know,
you have a heart that's true indeed.

So I guess what I'm doing
    is trying to say thank you
for accepting me for me

And not letting the reasons
    that have brought me here
be the man in me you see.

So as time progressed
    and someone asked
who wrote these words that are so sincere,

You be sure to tell them
    in whatever manner that suits you
that Andre Lawrence was here.

So where this journey takes me
    I boldly go
until the day I'm finally free.

And I'll never forget
    all the wonderful
people at Rochester FMC.

Uniquely worded by
Andre "Doc" Lawrence

Nurse Appreciation Week

Here's to all of you
    for a job well done,
For enduring the battle
    until the battle is won,

For being the first line of defense
    in our medical field
And your dedicated service
    that never yields.

You are our best leading example
    of human display,
Though your sacrifice goes unnoticed
    throughout the course of the day.

Doc's Poetry Parlor

Whether you're giving a bath
    or passing out pills,
Changing dirty diapers
    or feeding guys meals,

You get the job done
    in such a unique way
That honor and praise
    we extend you this day.

So to all of you nurses,
    the old and the new,
We appreciate you and thank you
    for all that you do.

Happy Nurse Week!

Uniquely worded by
Andre "Doc" Lawrence

The Dearly Departed Son

The untimely news
    of your tragic death
put my emotions in a downward fall.

And I was forced to reflect
    the life and time of your father,
and his death I would recall.

The loss of him
    is still a wound unhealed
and a burden I still bear.

But to now come face-to-face
    with the death of his son,
I'm somewhat lost and in despair.

For I know the life
    the father embraced
was not meant to be repeated in his son.

The son was the future
    and meant to be an example
of the better things to come.

But fate has been dealt,
    and this young life is lost,
dimming the legacy of my dearest friend.

So my mourning is now double,
    and it's hard to hold back
all the pain I suffer within.

Now in light of this tragedy,
    we must all do our best
to get through the day-to-day.

And each sunrise and set,
    may he share it with us
that his memory never fades.

Uniquely worded by
Andre "Doc" Lawrence

A Mother I Have Never Met

Today I pay tribute
    and extend the highest honor
to a mother I have never met.

But I had you as an example
    of what she must've been like,
so I got a glimpse of what to expect.

And from what I've gathered,
    she was an amazing woman
who indeed held her own.

And she was fearless in the sense
    if you rubbed her the wrong way,
she had no problem making it known.

As I think of this mother
    whom I've never met
and all that I wished she'd known,

That there exists a man
    whom she would have loved to call son
and love like her very own.

But seeing that the opportunity has passed
    for us to ever meet,
I remain grateful for the gift you left.

And the memory of you
    will live on through the family
and overshadow your untimely death.

So in my final farewell,
    know that I love you
as I bow my head as a sign of respect.

Rest in peace, dear Mother,
    and you'll always be missed;
sincerely, the son you have never met.

Uniquely worded by
Andre "Doc" Lawrence

Eternally Whitney

So emotional am I
    as I express
these words within,

For through these words,
    my life will unfold
from the beginning to its untimely end.

See, I was a true Jersey girl
    raised by my mother;
the church choir is where I got my start.

But already having family on the scene
    and being the goddaughter of a queen,
I knew music was where I'd make my mark.

And sure enough,
    as I embraced my dream,
I found fame on the other side.

But none of it would've been possible
    be it not for the man
and friend I found in Clive.

See, as a team, we went on
    to create such hits like
"You Give Good Love" and the "The Greatest Love of All."

And when I strayed off course
    and my world began crashing,
he was there to cushion my fall.

Now looking back on my life,
    I can't help but recall
those I've touched and the joy it brings.

But I've known no greater joy
    than the day I gave birth
to my daughter, Bobbi Christine.

Yeah, I'm sure
    there will be some who'll say
what a shame how I cast my life's lot.

But in the end of life's tale,
    we're all simply human,
and I would ask them to judge me not.

Instead, remember me so
    for my lyrical flow
and how my music brought you delight.

And now that I'm gone,
    let my legacy live on,
for this angel has taken flight.

Uniquely worded by
Andre "Doc" Lawrence

In Memory of Li'l Arthur

Today once again,
    we lay to rest
one of our very own,

Another senseless tragedy
    to transpire in the streets
within the borders of our home.

For all in an instant,
    he made the transition,
going from dark to light.

No farewells
    or "Holler at me later,"
he was swiftly stripped of life.

Death came with force
    with only a second to breathe
before it finally settled in.

In his untimely death,
    he leaves many to mourn,
a host of family and friends.

But let us turn his death,
    no matter the reason,
into a life lesson we swear to keep.

And let us never forget
    and say his name with honor
as we lay our brother to sleep.

Now we say our goodbyes
    with tear-filled eyes
and do our best from this point to be strong.

And healing will come in time,
    and thoughts of you will cross our mind,
and your memory will always live on.

Uniquely worded by
Andre "Doc" Lawrence

O Mother My

O Mother my,
    allow me to express in words
and relieve you of the question why,

For I know it mourns your soul
    and weighs heavily upon you
that death wouldn't pass me by.

But rest assured
    that even in death,
our love will continue to grow.

Though the timing was sudden
    and without fair warning,
the outcome was in God's control.

So be strong for me
    and our family
and stay focused on things on high.

And know the day will come,
    sure as the rising sun,
we'll meet again, O Mother my.

Uniquely worded by
Andre "Doc" Lawrence

In Memory of Rachel

Today the clouds
    of sorrow gathered
and greeted me with a storm of pain.

And with no warning at all,
    a precious soul was lost,
and life forever changed.

So in disbelief
    and total shock
at the news I received from home,

I must find a way
    to accept this truth
that my daughter is truly gone.

Now as I wrestle and fight
    through these endless nights
at the revelation of my current state,

I pray God will have mercy
    and keep me strong
and strengthen me in my faith.

And as I prepare for the future,
    I look forward to my healing
and the promise of better days.

Rachel, your death was untimely,
    and in my heart is where I'll keep thee
and love you always.

Uniquelyworded by
Andre "Doc"Lawrence

For Royal

Dearly Beloved

Dearly beloved,
    we have been called to gather
to honor the legacy of a phenomenal man

Whose life's work
    is truly transcending,
and the test of time it shall withstand.

For from an early age,
    he had a passion for music
that he maintained ever since.

In the movie, he was the kid,
    and for a time, he was the symbol
but is affectionately known as Prince.

He gave us electric hits
    such as "Let's Go Crazy"
that kept us on our feet.

And when our hearts were heavy,
    he gave us "Purple Rain"
to hide the tears we often weep.

Dearly beloved,
    we mournfully grieve
our precious purple one,

Who, from the stage at First Avenue,
    did something spectacular
that will never be undone.

So now there's no doubt
    that doves will surely cry
in light of the passing great.

But what he has given of his gift
    will always remain
and never fade away.

Uniquely worded by
Andre "Doc" Lawrence

Trina Lives

Having had my last dance,
    I have taken my bow
and moved on to my eternal place.

Not that the choice was mine,
    but here I have served my time,
because if I could, I would rather stay.

But for reasons unknown,
    it's God who sits on the throne,
and it's his will that shall be done.

And though he has called me home,
    you'll never be alone;
I am with you constantly like the rising sun.

So let not your hearts be troubled,
    causing your souls to mourn
in my absence as you think of me,

For I am Trina, the beloved,
    a mother to all,
and I live on eternally.

Uniquely worded by
Andre "Doc" Lawrence

The Last of the Leading Ladies

Lula's firstborn girl
> withstood life's test
and endured 'til her very last breath.

She was a mother, a wife,
> and the love of all who knew her
and will remain so even in death.

For oh, how fast
> did the hands of time turn
as you sojourned through this thing called life.

From your very first breath,
> you accomplished all that you could
before the day your soul took flight.

So now there will be
    no more struggles, sickness, and pain,
no more worries or constant stress.

You lived life well,
    being the best woman you could;
now the Lord has given you rest.

So rest now, Dorothy,
    and bear no concern
for those you leave behind.

And though you're gone,
    it's only in the physical,
for your memory will transcend time.

Uniquely worded by
Andre "Doc" Lawrence

Time after Time

Time after time,
    we mournfully gather
to say goodbye to a loved one gone.

And in their absence,
    in light of all that happened,
we must somehow carry on.

Because life for us,
    we will not stand still,
allowing us only a moment to grieve.

And try as we must
    to be not consumed by sorrow,
the pain will never leave,

For the loved one lost
    is a loss too great,
like robbery of the cruelest kind,

For the life was short-lived,
    full of potential and promise,
but another future that has been denied.

So now candlelight vigils
    will be our constant reminder
to ensure the memory never fades.

And though we suffered a loss,
    we will grow stronger
and live fuller with each waking day.

Uniquely worded by
Andre "Doc" Lawrence

Inspired by the tragic death of my young cousin Devon
Kawana's son

Eternally Uncle Lewis

Today we gather
    to honor the life and memory
of a man we all hold dear,

A man whose presence
    will be forever felt
even though he's no longer here,

A man who's faithful
    to answer the call
and always made a showing,

Who endured a full life,
    weathered the good and bad,
and showed no signs of slowing,

Whose life and legacy
    continue to excel
through the lineage of his daughters and sons.

And though we lay you to rest,
    Uncle Lewis, you were the best
and will always be our number one.

Uniquely worded by
Andre "Doc" Lawrence

I Am Muhammad Ali

It seems it's curtain call
    and this warrior's down,
And death is the victor
    in this last final round.

My life was a grand spectacle
    for all eyes to see;
I only pray I lived a life worthy
    of you all remembering me.

Though I was known as the greatest
    to ever enter the ring,
Without family and faith,
    it wouldn't mean a thing.

Family was the motivation
    from which my journey begins,
But my faith has been my comfort
    up until my untimely end.

And fearless as I was
    when fighting a match,
My love for the people
    could double that.

Having bore witness to our struggle,
    I was left without choice;
Seeing that my people had been silenced,
    I became their voice,

Taking on new opponents,
    those of the political field,
Demanding justice and equality
    so that my people could heal,

With hopes of ensuring our legacy
    as a people would stay strong
And deeds of our ancestors
    throughout generations would pass on.

Having best filled my duty
    in this life, I'm now free,
The last to float like a butterfly
    and sting like a bee.

    I Am Muhammad Ali.

Uniquely worded by
Andre "Doc" Lawrence

In Loving Memory of Li'l Greg

Alone I sit
    in utter silence
as I absorb this tragic news.

It seems that in my absence,
    there is no end
to the loved ones I am to lose.

For death has made
    an untimely visit,
leaving another household stunned.

Now I search for words
    to comfort my brother
who has lost his firstborn son.

So now family and friends
    shall once again gather
to mourn this life that is now gone.

They will say their goodbyes
    and offer encouragement
to the sad sound of monotones.

Such a bitter fate
    to die so young
and for a cause that remains unknown.

He'll transcend
    to that heavenly realm,
and his name we'll etch in stone.

His memory in life
    we'll always have,
and I'm sure we'll heal in time.

And I pray these words
    comfort you, Greg and Sherell
and the loved ones he leaves behind.

Uniquely worded by
Andre "Doc" Lawrence

Breathing through the Storm

Today a storm has come
    to trouble me some,
bearing nothing but the gift of grief.

So now my family mourns
    another lost to death,
that ever-consuming beast.

In between the anguish of pain
    and tear-filled eyes,
I fight to catch my breath,

For though my nephew is gone,
    I know the day shall come
when I too shall face this death.

But for now I focus
    and remain that beacon of strength
to help my family maintain the norm,

Knowing as time goes by
    and new dark clouds come,
I will continue breathing through the storm.

Uniquely worded by
Andre "Doc" Lawrence

In loving memory of my nephew Darion

Mildred's Son

They say in life,
    what will
shall surely be.

God grants us life
    that we may live
with death as the only certainty.

And without a moment's notice,
    heaven opened its doors
and welcomed your spirit home.

No more days of pain,
    struggles, and sorrow;
you're in the presence of the heavenly throne.

Although your death was untimely
    and more than shocking,
your presence here still lives on.

You weren't just my mother
    but a champion in life
and the family's true cornerstone.

You open your heart
    and the doors to your home
to those who didn't have enough.

You've given more of yourself
    than you'll ever know,
and it's reflected in those you've touched.

Now in light of the reality
    life has dealt me
one that cannot be undone,

Though I mourn for the moment,
    I will live on
for I am Mildred's son.

Uniquely worded by
Andre "Doc" Lawrence

Before the Heavenly Trumpet Blows

Comfort me now,
    O Heavenly Father,
and grant strength in my hour of need.

Though I am unprepared
    to let this love go,
to your will I do concede,

For all things are yours
    that are in heaven, in earth,
and for every soul you have a plan.

You saw it pleasingly fit
    to call Momma home;
though I mourn, I understand.

As an expression of your love,
    you granted us time
that in this life we may come to know

That we should cherish each moment
    with those we love
before that heavenly trumpet blows.

Uniquely worded by
Andre "Doc" Lawrence

In the Blink of an Eye

It's within that blink of an eye
    that life has been lost
and situations are now rearranged.

My friend is now gone,
    and I am forced to move on,
but life will never be the same.

"Here one day
    and gone the next"
is an expression we all know and feel.

So with a sense of urgency,
    we move through life
with hopes of outliving what time will reveal.

When the hand of death knocks,
    no one wants to answer,
yet its course can't be undone.

Sadly, death came knocking
    and called on the soul
of someone I knew and loved.

So to the family and friends
    with whom I share in mourning,
like you, my heart shall grieve.

But the memory of him,
    who was more like a brother,
will never flee from me.

So with our heavy hearts
    and tear-filled eyes,
we look to you within the sky,

Vowing never to take life
    or those we love for granted
because it can be lost in the blink of an eye.

    In the blink of an eye.

Uniquely worded by
Andre "Doc" Lawrence

Let It Be Said

Let it be said
    that I lived this life
down the path I chose my own.

And I have no regrets
    though mistakes were made,
for through them, I have grown.

Let it be said
    that my love knew no bounds
for my family and friends who mourn.

And to my mother, I say
    I know you're hurting this day,
but find the strength to endure and go on.

Let it be said
    before the end of my life's journey,
I made an impression on those I knew.

So I know without doubt,
    as life moves on,
my legacy will live on through you.

Let it be said
    when my eulogy is read
in the presence of all who attend my wake,

Though my death was untimely,
    in your hearts you'll still find me
for I have moved on to a peaceful place.

So it's farewell for now,
    and I hope you find peace
with the fact I'm no longer here.

But know in your heart,
    though we're physically apart,
in spirit I'm always near.

Uniquely worded by
Andre "Doc" Lawrence

Love eternally,
Li'l Pat

I Am Still Here

As elusive as time can be,

Though separated in the physical,
    you were never far from me.

Though young,
    our feelings developed a stronghold,

Warmly embracing the heart
    only to penetrate the soul,

That as life moved forward,
    we would remain inseparable
despite the lapse in time.

And though the roads of our lives
    took their separate course,
our souls remained intertwined,

That in the absence
    of our physical presence,
the memory would never fade,

Of who we are,
    what we shared,
and the impact that was made.

Now having come full circle
    after being worlds apart,
as the days went from months to years,

I pray you find comfort in the fact
    despite all that has transpired
that I am still here.

And there's no rhyme or reason
    to the question why,;

Just search that sacred place
    despite the lapse in time,

And I'm certain there
    you're sure to find
me,

Because a home for you my heart has built
    to always keep you near,

And if it must be said
    as time moves ahead,

You are the reason
    that I am still here.

Uniquely worded by
Andre "Doc" Lawrence

Endlessly Fateful

Oh, how beautiful
    fate has become
by allowing this reconnect.

Now my heart sings a song
    and pounds deep within
due to the intoxicating effect,

For it seems you've suffered
    a life of torment
in that long absence of you

And each waking day
    was a trial in itself
just to make it through.

But it appears destiny's hand
    would change infavor
of a love that's proven true

And all roads in life
    were aligned to a course
that would lead me back to you.

But with all we've endured
    in our separate lives
and the moments we were out of touch,

I'm excited to see
    what the future holds
and what shall become of us.

And though we both bear scars
    and emotional wounds
by those who should've loved us back,

I need you to know
    no matter how things go,
this love will always be intact.

Uniquely worded by
Andre "Doc" Lawrence

Alone with My Thoughts

From the start of my day,
    at the rising of thesun,
my desires come alive.

My first thought is you
    then your touch
and the feeling of your inner thighs.

As the desire builds,
    it fills my body,
leaving me hard and warm.

And my only relief
    is when I have you near
to soothe me like a quiet storm.

At your discretion,
    I surrender my flesh
to be used as you so please.

And I give you my word,
    as we build on our trust,
I'll become all you'll ever need.

Uniquely worded by
Andre "Doc" Lawrence

Look at Me

Look at me;
    no, seriously, look at me!
Is not my presence and sum of worth
    not clear for the eye to see?

Look at me
    and not just through me,
And know I'm not some hollow shell
    of what you would have me to be.

Look at me
    and share with me your thoughts;
If you will allow me to, I'll be your support and strength
    and will prevail at any cost.

Look at me
    through the window where my soul resides,
Where no secrets harbor and only love exists
    and will never be denied.

Look at me
    when you're lost, confused, and alone,
Because I'll be that light in the darkest night
    to safely guide you home.

Look at me
    and know my existence is true;
Trust in me, and in time, you'll see
    that I'll always be there for you.

    Look at me.

Uniquely worded by
Andre "Doc" Lawrence

Love's Devotion

Spare me nothing in life
    that consists of you
no matter what shall be revealed in time.

Be it love or pain
    you choose to render,
I'll accept and never decline.

For my heart and soul
    will never turn cold
and my sleeve has never worn my pride,

Being that it's you who sustains me
    and I am ever consumed
by the warmth of you inside.

If only time would stand still,
    I'd express all that I feel
of the many ways because of you, I am more,

Though I have had some experience
    and a broken heart or two,
but never a love like you before.

And there is no greater reward
    I have ever known
than those moments I shared with you.

So if it should ever arise
    that I should have to walk down that aisle,
I'd gladly say I do,

Because what you have given me
    is more than special;
it is precious and hard to find.

Many have searched for this love
    that everyone knows
comes once in a lifetime.

Uniquely worded by
Andre "Doc" Lawrence

Loving You in Hindsight

Today I said farewell
    to a longtime love,
so it seems time is standing still.

And suddenly, I'm rushed
    with all the moments we shared,
so I pray in time, I'll heal.

Now looking back on the course
    of our relationship shared,
I can see the errors of my foolish ways.

I only showed you neglect
    and appreciated you less,
causing you to slowly change,

Change from the woman
    who was love's sacrifice,
who loved me over everyone else.

But I failed to return
    that love you deserved,
and you were forced to live and love yourself.

No one told me
    how much letting go hurts,
so I'm new to this emotional strain.

But in my seclusion,
    alone with my feelings,
I'm forced to feel your pain.

And what a lesson I learned,
    painful no doubt,
in the conclusion of what became of us.

So I guess in my absence
    and our lack of communication,
it appears I've given up.

I didn't give up onlove
    or you, for that matter,
because our relationship ceased to work.

I just loved from a distance
    and stayed out your business
so neither of our feelings would get hurt.

Uniquely worded by
Andre "Doc" Lawrence

One-Sided Love

We entered this thing
    with a common goal,
and I never left your side.

You were my king
    and ruled my world
for I was your loyal bride.

Through thick and thin,
    the good and bad,
my devotion never faded.

But as time progressed,
    you showed love less,
leaving me scared and jaded.

I contemplated awhile
    on thoughts within,
on where our love lost its spark,

Recalling how we started as a team
    and all the issues in between
I should leave but surrendered to my heart.

So I took a leap of faith
    to give our love a chance
with hopes we'll make it through.

But all was made clear,
    and you confirmed my fears
that it was me who was only loving you.

You chose to use and abuse
    and take for granted
a love so true and kind.

So now it's "So long"
    for I have moved on,
and my love you'll never find.

Uniquely worded by
Andre "Doc" Lawrence

A Song to Memory

Every time I hear
    a certain song,
my mind begins to race,

And memories flash
    of my histories past
to that all-familiar place,

To that place in time
    when you were mine
and life was worry-free,

When our love was grand
    and I was your man
and your heart belonged to me.

As the song plays on,
    the memory grows strong,
and visuals become clearer to view,

And my breathing quickens
    as part of me stiffens,
as I envision making love to you.

Breathless and without words,
    I'm detached from the present;
the vision leaves me suspended in time.

Then suddenly, a breath is taken,
    and from this state I awaken
to the realization of my shameful crime,

That true love was my fortune found
    and, like a fool, I played the clown
and squandered this love away.

So now my mind will always race
    and I'll be frozen in time
when I hear that certain song play.

Uniquely worded by
Andre "Doc" Lawrence

Senses

With just one look,
    you're sure to know,
for the eyes will tell no lie.

With just one touch,
    you'll feel the rush
and a feeling you can't deny.

With just one kiss,
    your fate is sealed
as your desires take full control.

And try as you must
    to suppress your hunger of lust,
the anticipation has taken its toll.

So now you find yourself
    in an erotic scene,
experiencing pleasure you've never known.

And your body lies awake
    in a blissful state
as you passionately release a moan.

Uniquely worded by
Andre "Doc" Lawrence

Fears of Love

Loving you
    is my greatest joy and pain
all in the same breath,

Because to have you
    and not have you
is like a slow and painful death,

One I'd gladly die
    a thousand times
for the freedom to love you whole.

Every extreme would be met
    with no regret
to relieve my aching soul.

And though there be no doubt
    of your love for me,
circumstances keep us bound.

But we both know
    there's no force known
that could destroy what we have found.

But the question remains,
    with predictable outcomes
of them one must choose,

Do you live the life
    and willingly sacrifice
a love you can't stand to lose?

How unbearable then
    life would be
if likened to unread books on a shelf,

For in that moment, you have found love
    But, for fear,
could not have it for yourself.

Uniquely worded by
Andre "Doc" Lawrence

I Need You

I need you,

Not only when the storms of life
    have run their course
'til only a shell of who I am is left,

For you have been my strength,
    and there have been countless times
you've revived my soul from death.

I need you,

Like the body needs air to breathe,
    and without air, the body will die,
and without you, I am incomplete.

I need you,

Though at times I scream and shout,
    giving you reason to doubt
and burden your heart with grief,

But in and of myself,
    I am chaos complete
without you to show me peace.

I need you,
    just like the flowers
need rain and sun to bloom,

Like every unborn child
    before their birth
finds safety in their mother's womb.

I need you,
    though I'm certain
I can make it alone,

But the absence of you
    makes life twice as hard
and even harder to carry on.

I need you!

Uniquely worded by
Andre "Doc" Lawrence

Hello, Love

Hello, love,
    this love of mine
that I've loved from the very start,

Whose world I yearn
    to be in evermore
and presence to never part.

Though in times past,
    I've tried to deny you,
and it was all to no avail,

And though it took me a moment,
    I realized such an act
is the greatest self-betrayal.

Because love is eternal,
    boundless, and free
and on a course all its own,

It cannot be harbored,
   stored, or hidden,
and its limits are beyond unknown.

For time has proven
   that life without you
has been more than I can bear.

It was as if my soul
   separated from mybody,
leaving only a shell of me standing there.

So I say now, love,
   hello again,
and I'm glad to find you here.

And I know moving forward
   through all of life's trials,
I'll always have you near.

Hello, love

Uniquely worded by
Andre "Doc" Lawrence

Hearts Broken Silence

There's a sense of urgency
    running through me
as if I'm running out of time.

And no remedy known
    can console my soul
aside from making you mine.

Time and chance
    are one and the same
that have brought our worlds together.

And whatever the cause
    that has brought about the effect,
I choose to part from you never.

There is no value
    I could place upon
what my heart will never trade.

It surrendered whole
    and won't let go,
and the desire will never fade.

For you are that woman
    who has ignited more than flames
and has helped keep the man in me alive.

I know no other gift worth having
    than you as my queen
and always at my side.

So now I have said in words
    what my heart has hidden
and my tongue never spoke.

You are what Iwant,
    and to someday have you
is all that I can hope.

Uniquely worded by
Andre "Doc" Lawrence

I Am Torn

I am torn in two
    with my thoughts of you
as I reflect on what we once had.

We have shared a life
    that was filled with so much good
but has regretfully become our past.

So I question the fate
    of our present state,
or should I accept the blame as mine?

Or is what we've become
    just a numerical sum
of what was to be in time?

They say some grow together
    while others fall apart
for reasons that remain unknown.

You went from a summer breeze
    to a winter freeze,
and your heart has turned to stone.

Yet I am still torn
    in every way, shape, and form,
and my heart is filled with gloom.

It's as if part of me died
    and chose to take refuge
in the confines of an earthen tomb.

It's likened to
    an aborted child
removed from its mother's womb,

Disconnected
    and left desolate
for death to consume.

Yet in the absence of you,
    in this life I'll get through,
though my heart will always mourn.

And whatever the future unfold
    will remain untold;
until then, I am torn.

Uniquely worded by
Andre "Doc" Lawrence

Dreamland

Now I lay me
    down to sleep,
And thoughts of you
    I vow to keep.

For the day is done
    and I have done my best,
And now I prepare to drift
    into a peaceful rest.

I embrace my sleep
    with no despair,
Knowing in the realm of dreams,
    I'll find you there.

And it's here we're both
    worry-free
And bear no concerns
    for what shall be,

At liberty to explore
    each other's hidden depths,
And the freedom to indulge
    until there's nothing left.

So after endless consumption
    of you, I'm weak,
Then I awake but await
    the next time I sleep.

For in my dreams,
    it's you I hold,
And all we have
    cannot be told.

Awake in life,
    our hearts will weep,
So I long for the hours
    I lie down to sleep.

Uniquely worded by
Andre "Doc" Lawrence

Tell Me

Tell me those things
   that no one knows,
and safe with me they'll always be.

And not time or chance
   or life circumstance
would undo your trust in me.

I'll guard your heart
   and uplift your soul
and be a light when you're lost and empty

And provide what's needed
   to keep you whole
as if God himself has sent me.

Being at your side
   to support you through
whatever shall come your way

Is the motivating force
    that keeps me going
and propels me through my day.

So before the day has come
    to its dawning end
and I drift to quiet sleep,

I give thanks for the gift
    God has given me in you,
and your heart I'll always keep.

Uniquely worded by
Andre "Doc" Lawrence

Dual Inspiration

If you ask, I'm ready
    to do the unthinkable
to see where these feelings will go,

Though there is personal risk
    with feelings like this,
but to back out, we'll never know.

And I'm not the one
    to let the moment pass;
I'd rather seize it and fully live.

And for a chance
    at true romance,
all of me I'll truly give.

Some people want it all,
    and in this case,
those words ring loud and true,

Because this world and everything in it
    would be nothing
if I ain't got you.

For that particular woman,
    it may take a thousand lifetimes,
but one should never abandon the search.

And I'd gladly endure it
    to behold my *queen*
because I know a woman's worth.

The sound of your voice
    is like an intimate ringtone,
and my heart just keeps on calling.

Being the woman you are
    with beauty beyond measure,
I can't help but keep on falling.

And no matter how deep
    this rabbit hole goes,
I'll endure to the journey's end.

I see that you wear a ring
    and already have a king,
so I'll settle for being a friend.

Uniquely worded by
Andre "Doc" Lawrence

Where Are You Headed?

The first fruits of mankind,
    half human, half divine,
but how far have you fallen from grace?

Now your role remains void,
    while others seek and destroy,
and a nonentity has become your fate.

Where are you headed?

In a land among those
    who have found suitably fit
to be deemed the lesser than,

Not ever once giving thought
    to who you are, who you could become,
or who you might have been.

Where are you headed?

In the midst of a society
    that perpetuates your demise
under the guise of law and order,

When, truth be told,
    they'd rather lay waste of your soul
and that of your sons and daughters.

Where are you headed?

Living wild in the streets,
    roaming to and fro,
killing, and selling what can be sold.

But this is a fool's games end—
    one outcome is the pen;
the other, a rotting corpse cold.

Andre Lawrence

Where are you headed?

Having endured the prison term
    and freedom now yours,
you head for that place called home.

Your destination, once arrived,
    you see so much has changed with time
that you start to feel alone.

Where are you headed?

The ever proud and strong man
    whose destiny is at hand
of the people you were born to lead,

You were called to a purpose
    to uplift the lost and worthless
and be the example that nations shall heed.

Where are you headed?

In your quest of thought,
    in search of something more of meaning,
you pursue it from night 'til day.

Having overcome the odds,
    you pray and thank God,
knowing with him, you'll find your way.

Uniquely worded by
Andre "Doc" Lawrence

What Will My Legacy Be?

Today I ask
    myself the question,
what will my legacy be?

Will I leave this earth
    without having contributed something worthy
of others remembering me?

True reflection is needed
    to answer this question,
so I dived into my past,

Recalling each moment
    I've experienced in this life
from the first until the last.

My first recollection
    as an adolescent child,
I guess I was around the age of five.

I can see myself clearly,
    a younger version of me
in the dirt making mud pies.

Fast-forward a little
    to my teenage years
where my life had taken a turn.

I'm at a crossroad in my life
    with no guidance in sight,
so I'm forced to live and learn.

And learn I did;
    I'm sixteen with a kid,
and the streets I constantly roam.

The streets are filled with tension;
    bad decisions led to prison,
so now a 6×9×12-foot cell is home.

But I'm young with heart
    and hella smart,
so I do the time without missing a beat.

Andre Lawrence

Though I stayed out the way
    and got my GED,
I discovered I learned more about me.

Moving right along
    to that point in my life
where the streets proclaimed my fame,

See, now I'm the boss
    calling all the plays,
and Dogg Pound is the set I claim.

At this point in life,
    I'm trying to do right
for death has taken its toll.

I still hear the cries
    and see the teary eyes,
for the losses still pains my soul.

My name hails great
    in the heart of the streets,
for none other could've played my role.

I was a leader for the people,
    allowing everyone to breathe
without imposing my control.

Final reflection
    as I look back on my life,
the error of my ways
    and the wrongs I made right.

My maturity is evident
    and plain to see,
and I made great strides in improving me.

But the question remains
    at the end of life's game,
what will my legacy be?

Uniquely worded by
Andre "Doc" Lawrence

I Am Atoning

I am atoning for the wild young man
    who once was but is no more,
Who lived life's course with no remorse,
    and the rules he lived to ignore.

I am atoning for the man without a plan,
    and destruction is his legacy,
For he was a soulless seed from his youth,
    and the life he lived bears this truth,
And how unfortunate because he may never be
    the man he was meant to be.

I am atoning for the man who rolled alone,
    who made the streets his cornerstone,
Who wears a mask to hide the scars and pain
    and the memories of the home from whence he came.

I am atoning for the man whose kids cry out
    "Where's Papa? Where's Papa?" 'til their voices die out,
And while they cry themselves to sleep,
    Papa's caged in a 8×9×12-footsuite
Because this is his home; yeah, I am atoning y'all.

I am atoning for the man who abandoned his post,
    so now his position is void,

So now the streets play Daddy but bears no love,
    so our youth are easily destroyed.

And though it may not have been his plan
    to become such a man,
It's the reality he's left to face.

And win, lose, or draw,
    if he chooses the right route,
He can return to his state of grace.

I am atoning for the man
    whom in the mirror I see,
And I embrace the truth of what will be.

And as much as I would like
    to make every man's wrongs right,
I can only atone for me.

    I am atoning . . .

Uniquely worded by
Andre "Doc" Lawrence

Still I Rize

Still I rize,
    having seen the sadness
of broken homes,

Where mothers turn tricks
    and child talk slick
and Papa's a rollin' stone,

Rollin' from one house to the next,
    and each house heinfects,
maintaining that broken tone.

But still I rize.

Still I rize
    though the course has been one setback
and one downfall after another,

One heartache, one bad break after another,
    one lie or half-truth,
leaving me to trust none other.

But still I rize.

Still I rize, despite being counted out from the beginning
    and only a slim chance at winning, for the hardships I've
had to endure truly left their mark, and scars I still bear,
both mentally and physically, from being undereducated, unaccepted,
underfed, unfit, and yet unprepared to advance in a society that keeps
me under suspicion, all the while
being under pressure to adjust in a world where I am unappreciated.

But still I rize.

I've risen to the occasion
    of life's situations
no matter the issue at hand,

Vowing never to give in
    to life's temptations
or bow to another man.

I surpassed the standards
    that were set before me
and overcame every obstacle.

I've risen from the ashes
    of nothingness
and accomplished the impossible.

    Yet still I rize.

Uniquely worded by
Andre "Doc" Lawrence

A Tribute to Woman

There exists a long list
    of attributes
that are synonymous in describing you.

And to just call you mother,
    wife, or lover
doesn't testify to all you do.

We must dig deeper
    to appreciate you more
and never lose you from sight.

We must nurture your essence
    and respect your presence
and honor you in this life.

For countless years,
    you were abused,
and our words were so profane.

We called you bitch and whore
    and every other vile thing
in place of your God-given name.

On a daily basis,
    we tore you down
as fuel for our selfish pride.

We made you a stool
    instead of letting you rule
properly at our side.

We are indebted to you,
    so it's your forgiveness
we solemnly lie in search.

And our past transgressions
    were actions of a fool;
today we know your worth.

Andre Lawrence

And in moving forward,
    it's hard to envision
a world where there is no you,

For if you didn't exist,
    neither would I
because I can't be without you.

They say a nation
    can never rise higher than its woman,
so it's in you we shall invest our stock.

You are a combination
    of many things,
but a bitch is what you're not.

So as time progress,
    I pray I am mindful
to never make you feel less

But to elevate you as queen
    and include you in all things
and love you with my humanly best.

Uniquely worded by
Andre "Doc" Lawrence

The Black Woman

O precious pearl,
    thou mother of the world,
through whom all man is born,

You have birthed many nations
    from generation to generation,
but from that precious land, you were torn.

Born African free
    as God meant it to be,
you were hunted and trapped like game

Then stored on a ship
    to endure the long trip
to a land that was foreign and strange.

Final destination,
    the land of America;
upon your arrival, you're shackled in chains

Then put on display
    and, for a price, ushered away
and given an American name.

No longer in touch
    with your culture and such,
for the plantation is where you now reside,

Where you're raped at random
    at the slave master's hand,
yet you maintained dignity and pride.

For through you so
    was knowledge passed on
and transcended the course of time.

You fashioned your role
    at the risk of being sold
to keep intact the family's line.

How strong is thee
    who has endured such loss
and continued to strive this very day,

For in spite of her position,
    she rose above her affliction
and will never fade away?

Though her suffering knew no relief,
    she persevered in quiet strength,
so we must honor her as best we can,

For no human has been tried
    suffered and survived
like the almighty black woman.

                                    Uniquely worded by
                                  Andre "Doc" Lawrence

Poetic Response to Li'l Baby

If no one's there
    but you,
then where am I?

I'd rather be with you
    then on a constant loop
running inside your mind.

Damn the door
    and open the blinds;
the silhouette of your nakedness will do,

Because I'm fearless and bold,
    and the whole world can watch
as I make sweet love to you.

Doc's Poetry Parlor

R. Kelly's the man,
    but nothing sets the mood
like a hit from ole Keith Sweat.

There are a lot of ways
    I intend to love you
and leave you drippin' wet.

Don't close your eyes,
    watch me work,
and say my name, if you please.

I'll caress and touch
    way better than silk
and promise to never leave.

What reminds me most
    when I think of you
is the way you made me feel.

You carried my burdens
    and gave me love;
of it, I know it's real.

Now for the rest of the poem,
    I'll sum it up
and put it plain as it can be.

I see you're out of the box
    and don't mind touching yourself;
I need you to do that in front of me.

Uniquely worded by
Andre "Doc" Lawrence

The Familiar Stranger

After careful evaluation,
    I've come to the realization
to you I am an unknown.

I'm like a roaming lion
    cast out to sea,
out of place and alone.

And I bear no illusions
    of our moments shared;
the bond we built is strong.

And I will never question
    what we have found
all my life long.

For true it is,
    and what I feel
is certain as my God-given name.

try Parlor

n't"

Andre Lawrence

I believe love and loyalty
    are an inseparable duo
that never ever parts.

So when you say you love me,
    no matter how sincere,
I'm forced to question you,

Because to only say it
    is just words being spoken
without an active follow-through.

I wish my life experiences
    were somewhat gentler
and what I believe I could undo.

Then I free myself
    of these tormented feelings
I sometimes feel toward you.

For there have been lessons learned
    in our journey shared,
and some were all too real.

You taught me love can be
    motionless and void
and verbally invoked at will.

Painful though
    but true no doubt,
and there's no one to pity me,

Because you have convinced yourself
    some things in life
just aren't meant to be.

Uniquely worded by
Andre "Doc" Lawrence

www.ingramcontent.com/pod-product-compliance
Lightning Source LLC
Chambersburg PA
CBHW021423070526
44577CB00001B/36